By What Authority?

Volume 1 — The Argument in Brief

You have been reading edited scripture.

By What Authority? – The Argument in Brief
First public edition, May 2026.
This edition is complete as published; no ongoing update schedule is planned.

Cite as: *By What Authority* series, Chrestos (2026).
DOI: `10.5281/zenodo.20085840`

Dataset and analysis workbench:
`archive.org/details/by-what-authority-pauline-analysis-zip`

No institution. No publisher. Freely shared.

ISBN 978-1-7646729-5-5 (PDF)
ISBN 978-1-7646729-0-0 (hardcover)

IN THIS SERIES

Volume 1 — The Argument in Brief
The complete case in one sitting. All the core claims; the evidence condensed.

Volume 2 — How Paul's Letters Were Edited
The full forty-nine-chapter argument: textual evidence, patristic timeline, gospel analysis, and the strongest objections answered.

Volume 3 — The Chain from Scripture to Sovereignty
The institutional and legal consequence: from the editorial programme to the Doctrine of Discovery, the oath architecture, and the question the system cannot answer.

Companion A — The Verse-by-Verse Analysis
The complete adjudication record: signal codes, confidence scores, and manuscript evidence for every assessed passage. Designed for scholarly consultation.

Companion B — The Reconstructed Pauline Letters
The ten Pauline letters with the identified interpolations removed. A clean reading text. Use alongside Companion A for the evidence behind each excision.

Full series: `archive.org/details/by-what-authority-full-series`

SHORT READINGS

Standalone introductory documents — each addresses the argument from a specific starting point.

The Argument in Twenty Minutes — a self-contained introduction: the full case from the felt tension to the Doctrine of Discovery, no prior reading required
`archive.org/details/by-what-authority-argument-twenty-minutes`

For People Drawn to Christianity — those who sense something real but cannot accept parts of what the tradition became
`archive.org/details/by-what-authority-for-people-drawn-to-christianity`

For People Who Left the Church — those who walked away and wonder whether they left the right thing
`archive.org/details/by-what-authority-for-people-who-left-the-church`

For Lawyers — those who work with authority and want to know where it comes from
`archive.org/details/by-what-authority-for-lawyers`

For Those Concerned with Indigenous Sovereignty — those who want to understand the documentary root of the colonial claim
`archive.org/details/by-what-authority-indigenous-sovereignty`

For People Who Have No Religion — those who assume Paul has nothing to say to them
`archive.org/details/by-what-authority-for-secular-readers`

For Military Personnel and Oath-Takers — those who have sworn allegiance and want to know what they swore to
`archive.org/details/by-what-authority-for-military-oath-takers`

All volumes freely shared.
Verse-by-verse analysis dataset and workbench: `archive.org/details/by-what-authority-pauline-analysis-zip`

Contents

List of Figures

The Tension You Have Probably Already Felt

If you have read the Bible – or even heard it described – you may have noticed something that nobody talks about directly.

Something doesn't fit. Most people feel it. Almost nobody names it.

There is a God in one part of it who commands the destruction of entire cities. Who drowns armies. Who demands exclusive loyalty on pain of generational punishment. Who makes a wager in his own court that costs a righteous man his children, his wealth, and his health – to settle a point about loyalty.

He operates through law, covenant, and retribution. His relationship with his people is conditional. Obey and be blessed. Disobey and suffer.

Then there is a different God.

Love your enemies. Pray for those who persecute you. The Father makes his sun rise on the evil and the good and sends rain on the just and the unjust. The reach comes before the reckoning. Restoration is offered before anything has been done to earn it.

No transaction. No condition. No prior grievance.

These are not different moods of the same being having a good day and a bad day.

Something deeper is going on. The two halves of this tradition do not resolve into each other – not through development, not through metaphor, not through theological sophistication. The tension is structural.

One is law and conditional covenant. The other is grace without condition.

If you have felt this and been told not to worry about it – that God develops over time, or that the New Testament fulfils the Old in ways that resolve the tension – and if those explanations have never quite satisfied you –

The tension is real. And it has been named before.

What if grace isn't the exception to the rule – but the rule was the exception to grace?

> In the second century, a theologian named Marcion felt this tension so acutely that he identified it and named it. The institutional church expelled him and called his position heresy.

> This document argues that his question deserves a more honest hearing than it has received. Not because Marcion was certainly right — but because the evidence behind his question is stronger than most people have had occasion to examine.

That is where this inquiry begins: not with empire, law, or sovereignty, but with the textual tension inside Paul.

What started as a Pauline textual analysis — an attempt to read Paul's letters carefully, without assuming the received text was original — raised more questions than it answered. Following those questions honestly led somewhere unexpected: to the foundational instruments of colonial sovereignty, to the legal architecture those instruments created, and to the question that sits underneath all of them. This series is what that inquiry produced.

Something in the received text doesn't fit. Most people who have read the Bible have felt it. The Paul who writes "nothing can separate us from the love of God" and the Paul who commands submission to governing authorities do not sound like the same person. This short form names that tension, traces its origin, and follows where the tracing leads.

How This Inquiry Began

This series did not begin with the conclusions it now defends. It began with a smaller question.

In the course of reading Paul's letters carefully — not as an academic project but as someone trying to understand what the texts actually say — a problem became impossible to ignore. The Paul of Romans 7 and the Paul of Galatians 2 do not sound like the same person. The Paul who writes that the law is holy, righteous, and good and the Paul who writes that we were held in custody under the law until faith should be revealed are using the same vocabulary in incompatible ways. Something was wrong with the text.

The standard explanations — Paul changed his mind, Paul was speaking to different audiences, Paul contained multitudes — could not account for the specific shape of the inconsistency. The disagreements were not on peripheral matters. They were on the central question of what Paul thought the law was for and how it related to the new life he claimed to have entered.

That observation led to a small project of textual checking — Marcion's recension of Paul, the manuscript variants flagged in the standard critical apparatus, the patristic citations that disagree with the canonical text. The expected result was that some passages would emerge as clearly secondary and the rest would resolve. The actual result was that the secondary passages, when laid out together, all moved in the same direction. Every one of them tightened Paul's relationship to the Hebrew covenant, the Creator God, institutional authority, or established hierarchy. None moved the other way.

A pattern this consistent calls for explanation, even if it does not by itself settle the question. It also could not be ignored. So the question expanded: who would have benefited from making the changes, and when? The answer pointed to a specific institutional setting in the second century. So the question expanded again: what was that institution doing with the edited text once it had it? This second expansion led, eventually and reluctantly, to the political and legal consequences that Volume 3 traces — because the edited text turned out to be load-bearing not only for theological orthodoxy but for the legal architecture of European sovereignty over the next fifteen centuries.

That is not the conclusion the inquiry set out to find. It is the line of argument the author believes the textual evidence makes worth testing.

This origin matters for the reader in three ways. First, the volumes were not planned in their current order. They accreted as the inquiry forced new ground. Volume 2 and this volume address the textual question. Volume 3 addresses what that textual finding implied for institutional and political authority. Companions A and B provide the apparatus that makes the textual case checkable.

Second, each layer should be judged on its own evidence. The writer's obligation is to keep the textual case checkable at every step. The reader's obligation, in return, is not to accept or dismiss the textual case because of agreement or disagreement with the institutional argument that eventually follows from it.

Third, an inquiry of this shape can be wrong. The series is offered not as a settled treatise but as a documented investigation: here is what was found, here is the trail by which it was found, and here is what the reader is asked to check.

What the Difference Sounds Like

Before any methodology, before the timeline, before the argument: here is the problem stated as simply as possible. Two passages from what the church calls Paul's letter to the Romans. One is in the reconstructed text this series produces. One is not.

Romans 8:31–39 — in the reconstruction

"What then shall we say about these things? If God is for us, who can be against us? He who didn't spare his own Son, but delivered him up for us all, how would he not also with him freely give us all things? Who could bring a charge against God's chosen ones? It is God who justifies. Who is he who condemns? It is Christ who died, yes rather, who was raised from the dead, who is at the right hand of God, who also makes intercession for us. Who shall separate us from the love of Christ? Could oppression, or anguish, or persecution, or famine, or nakedness, or peril, or sword? No, in all these things, we are more than conquerors through him who loved us. For I am persuaded that neither death, nor life, nor angels, nor principalities, nor things present, nor things to come, nor powers, nor height, nor depth, nor any other created thing, will be able to separate us from God's love, which is in Christ Jesus our Lord."

Romans 13:1–2 — not in the reconstruction

"Let every soul be in subjection to the governing authorities, for there is no authority except from God, and those who exist are ordained by God. Therefore he who resists the authority, withstands the ordinance of God; and those who withstand will receive to themselves judgment."

Both passages have been in every manuscript of Romans since the fourth century. The first Paul has no use for governing authorities — his argument moves toward the claim that nothing in the created order, no power or principality, touches the relationship he is describing. The second makes submission to governing authorities a divine command carrying the threat of divine judgment for resistance. They can be read as the same person. The question this series asks is whether they should be, once the manuscript evidence has been followed to where it leads. What follows is that documented case.

How to Read This Series

By What Authority is three narrative volumes and two reference companions.

Two tracks, held separately. This series makes two distinct arguments that can be evaluated independently. The first is textual and historical: that several Pauline passages central to hierarchy, covenant continuity, and submission to governing authorities are later additions rather than original to Paul, and that later institutions made consequential use of those passages. The textual claim is argued in Volume 2; the institutional history is documented in Volume 3. The series asks whether those two records should be read together. The institutional side of that question – the papal bulls, the case law, the oath architecture – is in the primary record and does not require any theological commitment to evaluate.

The second is theological: on Marcion's reading, the pre-insertion Paul describes grace as something already given by the unknown Father before law, punishment, priesthood, or institutional permission enter the picture. This cannot be demonstrated from the same evidence. It is an interpretation of what the forensic residue points toward. If nothing in that theological reading resonates with you, the historical and legal case stands on its own. Readers who are not drawn to it are invited to treat every theological passage in these volumes as "Marcion's interpretation" rather than as a claim being made on them.

What this series establishes, argues, and reads

Established: the primary source documents this series traces – the papal bulls, Cook's instructions, Johnson v. M'Intosh and its successors, the constitutional oath architecture – are real and publicly verifiable. The Doctrine of Discovery is established legal history. No special framework is needed to check them.

Argued: the central textual claim – that key Pauline passages providing authority for institutional hierarchy and submission to governing authorities were added to Paul's letters, not original to him – is a minority scholarly position with significant independent evidence. Volume 2 develops this case in full. A reader who accepts the documented chain but not the textual argument keeps the historical case and loses the explanation of how the chain acquired its theological warrant.

Interpretive: what the authentic Pauline material was pointing toward – grace before debt, restored relationship before punishment, and access to God without an institution standing in the way. This is offered for the reader who receives it; it is separable for the reader who does not. This series argues that the foundational instruments it examines carried claims of authority that deserve renewed scrutiny. The question it opens – by what authority things should be governed going forward – is not resolved here.

Volume 1 – The Argument in Brief. The argument in one sitting. This is the right starting point. All the core claims are present; the evidence is condensed. Roughly ninety minutes.

Volume 2 — How Paul's Letters Were Edited. The full case in forty-nine chapters: the textual evidence, the patristic timeline, the gospel analysis, the Greek text, the thematic analysis, the strongest objections. Every claim made in Volume 1 is evidenced here.

Volume 3 — The Chain from Scripture to Sovereignty. The institutional and political consequence of the textual argument. Traces the chain from the editing of Paul's letters to the Doctrine of Discovery, the oath architecture that extends it, and the legal question the system has not answered. Can be read independently of Volumes 1 and 2.

Companion A — The Verse-by-Verse Analysis. The complete scholarly adjudication record: signal codes, confidence scores, and manuscript evidence for every assessed passage. Designed for scholarly consultation — not sequential reading by a general audience.

Companion B — The Reconstructed Pauline Letters. The seven authentic Pauline letters with the identified interpolations (passages inserted by later editors) removed. A reading text, not a scholarly edition. Use it alongside Companion A for the evidence behind each excision, or alongside the canonical text to see exactly what has been taken out.

This short form now uses its own consecutive chapter order. Cross-references to the longer works use volume names and chapter titles where possible.

A Note to the Reader

This is the short form. It is designed to be read in one sitting — roughly an hour and a half. It covers the core argument: what the tension is, who first named it, what the textual evidence actually shows, and what it means.

Nothing here requires prior knowledge of theology, Greek, or church history. Technical terms are briefly defined in parentheses at their first use in the text. Fuller definitions are in the Glossary appendix at the back. The argument proceeds step by step. Each step follows from the previous one.

If you finish this and want the full evidence — every verse, every signal, every objection answered — that is Volume 2: By What Authority — How Paul's Letters Were Edited. The verse-by-verse adjudication and manuscript-witness detail are in Companion A: By What Authority — The Verse-by-Verse Analysis. The Pauline corpus as a clean reading text, with the interpolations removed, is Companion B: By What Authority — The Reconstructed Pauline Letters. The institutional and political implication of the textual argument is Volume 3: By What Authority — The Chain from Scripture to Sovereignty. Chapter headings here use the short form's own sequence. When the longer works are needed, this volume points to them by title rather than relying on borrowed chapter numbers.

A note for readers who feel some hesitation approaching this material. The fear that engaging with it might carry a consequence — spiritual risk, divine displeasure — is worth naming directly. In the argument developed here, the unknown Father operates through pure non-transactional grace, without condition or penalty. He does not punish inquiry. The fear of divine punishment for reading an argument is itself the Creator's logic operating — the conditional, threat-based framework this document argues was layered onto an earlier text. If the orthodox reading is correct, careful textual examination of disputed manuscripts is standard scholarly practice that Christian theologians have engaged for centuries. Either way, reading is safe.

A note on how this work was made and why it is free. Most academic work on contested textual questions is produced inside institutions, published behind paywalls, and read by specialists who cite each other. The people who might most want to engage with this question — those who have felt the tension in the received text, those whose ancestors' land was claimed under the authority this document traces, those who have taken oaths in the architecture this document examines — rarely have access to the apparatus that would let them test the claims.

This project made a different choice. The full dataset is public. The analysis tools are public. Every signal weight, every adjudication criterion, every confidence calculation is documented and reproducible by anyone with a text editor. The PDFs are free. The licence allows unrestricted use and redistribution. There is no paywall between this argument and the people it most directly concerns.

That is not a publishing strategy. It is structurally consistent with what the document argues. The authentic Paul argues that grace precedes the transaction — that what the Father offers does not wait for qualification, institutional standing, or earned merit. This document is offered the same way. You do not need credentials to read it, to check it, or to extend it. It is available before you have done anything to earn it.

The institutional tradition this document examines secured its authority in part by controlling access to the text — Latin only, authorised interpreters, laypeople formally excluded from direct reading. This document does the opposite. The methodology is open. The data is open. If the argument is wrong, the tools to prove it are already in your hands.

Who Marcion Was

Marcion of Sinope was born around 85 CE in what is now northern Turkey. His father was reportedly the bishop of the local Christian community. He was a wealthy shipowner – educated and deeply serious about the theological questions his faith raised.

This matters. Marcion was not an outsider. He was the bishop's son, raised inside the tradition, formed by it before he broke with it. He knew the texts and the community's politics from the inside. When he arrived in Rome with his theological position, he wasn't presenting novelties – he was presenting conclusions drawn from the tradition's own sources. His expulsion was not the rejection of an outsider. It was the institution expelling someone who had grown up inside it.

Around 140 CE he travelled to Rome and joined the Roman Christian community. He made a substantial donation – equivalent to a significant fortune – to the community's treasury. He also brought with him a fully developed theological position that he presented for consideration.

His position was this: the God of the Hebrew scriptures and the Father Jesus revealed are not the same being. The Hebrew God is real – he made the physical world and governs it through law and justice. But he is not the ultimate reality. The Father Jesus revealed was completely unknown before Jesus. He operates through pure grace with no transaction, no covenant, no prior claim on anyone. Jesus was the celestial messenger of this unknown Father – entering the Hebrew God's world from outside it to reveal what had always been hidden.

The Roman church expelled him in 144 CE. They returned his donation. He founded his own communities which spread rapidly across the empire – from Rome to Syria, from North Africa to Mesopotamia. Marcionite communities survived for several centuries, some into the 5th century and possibly later in isolated regions.

What most readers do not know: virtually every major institutional feature of orthodox Christianity was built partly in reaction to Marcion. The four-gospel canon was assembled as a direct response to his single-gospel canon. The Acts of the Apostles was elevated to scripture to refute his Paul-only apostolic claim. The interpolated Pauline letters embed pro-Hebrew material the orthodox tradition needed Paul to carry. The man called a heretic helped shape the institution that called him one. A necessary qualification: this volume argues Marcion preserved an earlier form of Paul, not that his full theological system was original. Marcion was making a second-century argument in second-century categories; the textual case here is narrower – that the Catholicising (the second-century editorial programme that standardised the emerging orthodox canon) tradition added material that moves Paul in a single direction. A reader can accept the textual case without endorsing Marcion's full framework. The fuller treatment is in Volume 2 Chapter 22, "Marcion's Evangelion."

One question follows from this immediately: if Marcion's collection came first, why does none of it survive in its original form? The answer is institutional. After the church acquired imperial authority under Constantine, heretical texts were ordered surrendered and destroyed. Marcion's churches, spread across the empire for over a century, were dismantled. What survives of his text does so accidentally — preserved in the extended quotations of opponents who could not refute what they would not cite. The five books Tertullian wrote against Marcion are the primary reason we know what his version of Paul said. The scale of that response tells you the scale of the threat.

Paul's original letters face the same problem. We have no autograph for any New Testament document. Paul wrote approximately 50–64 CE; our earliest surviving Pauline manuscript is Papyrus 46, dated approximately 175–225 CE. More than a century of copying by communities with strong interests in what the letters said separates us from the source. The reconstruction this series builds cannot recover what Paul originally wrote. What it can do is document the pattern in what survived — and that pattern runs in one direction only.

What follows is the full argument compressed into its essential shape. Each point is unpacked in detail in the sections after this.

This Argument Is Not About the Past

Most readers come to this series expecting a theological dispute — an ancient argument about Jewish law and Christian grace, interesting to scholars, distant from modern life. That expectation is reasonable. It is also wrong in a specific way that matters before anything else is said.

The common assumption is that when Paul writes about "the law" he means the Torah — the Old Testament legal code, the rules and rituals of first-century Jewish practice. On that reading, Paul's argument against the law is a historical debate inside a tradition that no longer governs anything outside religious observance. It ended. It was settled. It is over.

This series argues that Paul is not only debating Torah interpretation. He is asking a more basic question: does belonging come after law-keeping, ritual standing, and covenant identity, or before them? On the reconstruction defended here, grace comes first. It is not earned by obedience, secured by circumcision, granted by priests, or lost when the account looks bad. This is not a claim that Paul was hostile to Jewish people, or that the Hebrew tradition was wrong on its own terms. The Hebrew tradition carried the Creator's covenant faithfully – honestly, systematically, and at great cost. That is precisely why the later editors could reattach Paul to it so easily: the rules, offices, punishments, and covenant tests were already there. The connection between Paul and the Hebrew framework is, across every passage this series examines, consistently located in the interpolated material. On the reconstruction defended here, Paul shows far less stake in that framework than the canonical text later came to suggest.

What Grace Means Here

Here, grace does not mean niceness, indulgence, or religious forgiveness. It means standing and belonging given before any account is opened. It is not granted by an institution, mediated by a priest, earned by repentance, purchased by apology, or secured by correct belief. If belief were required first, belief would become the last price of entry; Christ reveals grace, not a new gate.

That is why the contrast with orthodox Christianity matters. Orthodox Christianity asks what must be believed, confessed, mediated, paid, obeyed, or restored before standing is granted. Grace points the other way: standing was never the institution's to grant. The machinery of access is what later Christianity built around the thing this reading finds already given.

Practically, this does not erase responsibility. If harm has been done, truth and repair still matter. But responsibility is not there to settle a score; it is there to protect the harmed, tell the truth, and make repair possible. Forgiveness, if it comes, belongs to the harmed person. It is not owed to the one who caused harm and it is not purchased by an apology.

Orthodox Christianity vs Grace

The contrast below is not between true Christians and false Christians. Orthodox Christianity follows the received Bible, including the ledger-reopening themes named here. This series asks whether those themes belong to the earliest recoverable Pauline layer, or entered through the editorial process documented in Companion A and read continuously in Companion B.

The left-hand column is orthodox Christianity as received: law, judgment, mediation, hierarchy, birth-lineage continuity, and final accounting. The right-hand column is grace in the reconstructed Paul: standing before accounting, access without mediation, Christ sent and revealed without a birth narrative, and a relationship no ledger has jurisdiction over.

Orthodox Christianity	Grace in the reconstruction
Access is narrowed through gates, offices, rituals, belief, or final admission.	Grace has no gatekeeper. Standing is given before the account is opened.
Sin creates debt; confession, repentance, absolution, or forgiveness clears it.	Forgiveness may follow, but grace goes deeper: debt no longer names the person.
Law is fulfilled, moralised, or reintroduced as obligation.	The law's jurisdiction ends. Grace is not a better law.
Authority runs through church, priesthood, sacrament, canon, office, and doctrine.	Paul receives by revelation, not from men. No priest, office, council, or canon controls the way in.
Judgment becomes final accounting: who is in, who is out, who stayed worthy.	No condemnation. Nothing in creation can separate the believer from God's love.
Ethics prove standing; failure threatens it.	Ethics are fruit, not purchase. The fruit does not come before the root.
Hierarchy stabilises the community: husbands, masters, rulers, bishops, household codes.	No Jew or Greek, slave or free, male and female. The old categories lose their claim.

The law-and-covenant pattern Paul was resisting did not stay in the synagogue. It did not end in the first century. Paul named the first form of this pressure himself: Judaising. It came from Jerusalem, not Rome — from James and the circumcision party pressing covenant continuity against grace before any Catholic institution existed. What later became Catholicism scaled what Jerusalem had already established. The Catholicising editorial programme that reattached Paul to the law-and-covenant framework did so because the same pattern supported the institution's own authority: rank above equality, conditions before belonging, punishment after failure, command from above. That pattern became church government, then papal claims over kingdoms and territories, then the Doctrine of Discovery, then Crown title, colonial grants, and national sovereignty in the English-speaking world today. The standard constitutional law textbooks describe the chain openly. Volume 3 argues that the same law-centred architecture later visible in ecclesiastical and constitutional forms can be traced, in part, through the Pauline interpolations documented here. The institutional chain is documented there; the theological genealogy is the series' explanation of that chain.

As this series frames it, the textual argument does not stay within ancient religious history. If the passages identified here as interpolated are later additions, then the apostolic warrant they carry was not Paul's. What that means for the legal chain built on that warrant is the subject of Volume 3. This volume's task is to document the textual foundation that argument depends on. The passages that were inserted into Paul's letters – submit to governing authorities, silence women, restore covenant continuity, rank households – gave that law-and-covenant pattern an apostolic signature. The retained Pauline material, on this reconstruction, treats that pattern as already over: no condemnation, no Jew or Greek, no slave or free, no return to the yoke. The edited text restored apostolic support to an architecture the retained Pauline voice had treated as superseded. And the rebuilt version is what Volume 3 argues the legal chain has stood on ever since.

Volume 3 of this series traces the chain in detail. This volume documents the textual foundation the chain rests on. The question at the end of both is the same: if the apostolic authority for the law-and-covenant architecture was manufactured, what does that mean for everything built on top of it?

The Argument in Brief

A note before what follows. The Argument in Brief presents the transaction/grace contrast as the interpretive lens this volume defends. The framework is a reading drawn from a specific reconstruction of Paul (the Marcionite recension) tested against the structural and patristic (second- to fifth-century church writers who preserve the earliest external evidence about New Testament texts) evidence assembled in Volume 2. It is not a textual finding visible on the surface of the canonical text. A reader who does not accept the underlying reconstruction will not see the framework in the canonical Paul. A reader who accepts it will see it as the document's central organising claim. The distinction between the lens and the textual evidence on which it rests is preserved throughout this volume; it is named here so it cannot be lost.

What if the oldest recoverable layer of the Christian sources describes something so incompatible with the tradition that eventually canonised them that the tradition had to edit them to survive?

This document identifies transactional logic and grace at the centre of Christian origins – a transactional logic governing law, retribution and covenant, and grace, which is categorically different in kind. It argues that Paul's authentic letters describe grace in ways that cannot be harmonised with transactional logic, that the canonical tradition edited Paul to make them compatible, and that the original Pauline gospel was more radical than what survives. Marcion named the incompatibility as two Gods. This document treats that naming as a serious possibility rather than a foundational assertion.

The Theological Framework

- Transactional logic and grace run through the material this document examines. Transactional logic – law, retribution, hierarchy, conditional relationship – governs the world as it presents itself and underlies the Hebrew covenant system. Grace – non-transactional, unconditional, preceding repentance – is what Jesus made visible and Paul described in his authentic letters. These are not different moods of one being. They are categorically different in kind and resist every attempt to harmonise them without one being falsified. Marcion named them as two Gods. This document takes that naming seriously as a possibility the incompatibility points toward – held open rather than asserted. (Volume 2 Chapter 3, "Transaction and Grace")

- The unknown Father required revelation because no human religious imagination naturally produces a God of pure non-transactional grace. Every religious system humanity has independently generated operates through some form of exchange – obey and be rewarded, sin and be punished. A God who reaches the evil and the good alike with sun and rain, who arrives before any account of merit is rendered, is structurally antireligious. He had to be shown. (Chapters 1, 15) J. Louis Martyn – writing from within mainstream apocalyptic Pauline scholarship, not from any sympathy with Marcion – describes God's action in Galatians using almost identical terms: the gospel announces 'God's invasion of the cosmos' from beyond it, and 'the corresponding apocalyptic motif of divine invasion indicates his certainty that that universal state of enslavement has been broken only by God's movement into the human scene from beyond it.' An orthodox Pauline scholar reaches the same structural conclusion about the direction of the movement – from outside in, not from within out – through entirely different methodology.
- The celestial being sent by the unknown Father entered the Creator's domain under the conditions of flesh – encountered by the Creator's world as flesh, without the reconstruction supplying Bethlehem, genealogy, or miraculous conception. The Creator's instruments killed the flesh. The death was the release mechanism – the seed that dies to multiply. What was concentrated in one body distributed into universal availability. (Volume 2 Chapter 5, "Christ in the Flesh")
- The unknown Father does not intervene by forcing events: changing a verdict, stopping an army, suspending death, or making the world obey a new command. That would still be law, only with a different ruler. He acts instead by entering the place law cannot finally control: the person. Paul's phrase, Christ lives in me, is the concrete claim. Not Christ issuing orders from above, but Christ present within the one whom law can accuse, punish, or kill without reaching what has been given there.
- For Marcion, and for the argument developed here, the unknown Father's grace requires nothing to receive it. That is how Marcion defined the distinction: not a reward system, not a transaction, not a condition. It is the description of what an unconditional principle looks like when followed to its logical end.

Transaction and Grace at a Glance

Transaction and grace: the Creator's transactional logic – law, covenant, conditional – and the unknown Father's non-transactional logic – unconditional, reaching the evil and the good alike. The argument depends on holding them categorically different, not as moods of a single being. The textual evidence for what was done to Paul follows.

The Textual Evidence

- Paul's letters have been partially rewritten by the Catholicising tradition. The strongest cases – Romans 7, Romans 9–11, Romans 13:1–7, 1 Corinthians 14:34–35, 2 Corinthians 6:14–7:1, and 1 Thessalonians 2:14–16 – are identified by five core evidence tests working simultaneously, within the fuller twelve-code scoring apparatus used in Companion A: the passage disrupts the surrounding argument, the writing style shifts noticeably, it is absent from Marcion's earlier text, it first appears in anti-Marcionite controversy, and it serves a specific institutional need. The five tests are the readable summary; the twelve signal codes separate related forms of evidence so they can be recorded and weighted consistently. Several of these passages are also identified as non-Pauline by mainstream scholars who have never heard of Marcion. (Volume 2, "The Greek Text," "Romans," "Galatians," and the Pauline corpus chapters)
- Romans has a hidden architectural pattern – sections that mirror each other symmetrically, like a sentence that reads the same from both ends toward the middle. Its centre is Romans 8:1–17 – no condemnation, Spirit adoption, nothing separating from the Father's love. Three sections disrupt this symmetry: Romans 7, Romans 9–11, Romans 16:25–27. Romans 9–11 and Romans 16:25–27 are absent from Marcion's text; Romans 7 is identified as an interpolation through writing-style analysis independent of Marcionite evidence. All three show a writing-style shift from authenticated Paul. All three serve the institutional needs of the Roman church. The pattern is consistent with deliberate disruption of the letter's structure. (Volume 2 Chapter 6, "Romans")
- A note for readers who approach Romans 9–11 with a stake in the outcome. For many orthodox readers, Romans 9–11 carries Israel theology, election, and covenant continuity – and the assumption follows that removing it strips Paul of his most generous Jewish writing. The textual case in this volume is the opposite: Romans 9–11 is structurally paired in the ring model but expands asymmetrically into three chapters of dense

covenant-continuity material; its theology of conditional covenant and law-keeping sits in tension with the grace argument the surrounding chapters develop; and the chapters' removal produces what appears to be a cleaner rhetorical flow (Romans 8 ⟶ 12, with the 'therefore' of 12:1 now tracing back to 8:38–39 rather than across three intervening chapters). The full case is developed in Chapter 2 and in Volume 2.

- Across the strongest interpolation cases, the movement is consistent: toward law, hierarchy, covenant continuity, and institutional authority. That direction matters because it matches the textual-critical pattern Bart Ehrman documents in Orthodox Corruption of Scripture (1993): proto-orthodox scribal changes tend toward the dominant institutional theology rather than away from it.
- Galatians requires almost no reconstruction and produces the same theological system as reconstructed Romans. This independent convergence – one letter filtered, one letter transmitted nearly intact, both arriving at the same position – is the strongest evidence that the system is authentic Paul rather than a modern construction. (Volume 2 Chapter 8, "Romans and Galatians")
- The Roman church held physical custody of Romans and had both motive and opportunity to edit it. Letters held by communities outside Roman institutional control – Galatians, Philippians – show the least evidence of interpolation. Physical custody correlates with editorial intervention. (Volume 2 Chapter 40, "Rome, Custody, and Control")

The Gospel Tradition

- Marcion's Evangelion (his single gospel, related to canonical Luke but without the birth narrative or genealogy) – reconstructed through Tertullian's quotations by Jason BeDuhn, whose 2013 monograph The First New Testament: Marcion's Scriptural Canon is the standard scholarly edition – opens with Jesus appearing as a fully formed adult in Capernaum. No birth narrative, no genealogy, no Bethlehem, no childhood. In this reconstruction, the birth narratives are not what Marcion removed from an original. They are what later editors added – the content of the birth narratives (genealogy, Bethlehem, Jewish covenantal continuity) is precisely what a proto-orthodox editor would need to insert, not what a Marcionite would need to remove from a gospel already matching his theology. The unknown Father's revealer does not need a birth narrative. The Creator's messiah does. Paul's silence sharpens the point: if a virgin birth were already central proof of Jesus's identity, Paul had every reason to use it and never does. His Christ is sent, revealed, crucified, raised, and formed in the believer; he is not argued from Bethlehem, Mary, genealogy, or miraculous conception. That absence does not prove the birth narratives were invented later, but it makes their later function visible: they supply precisely the covenant-continuity apparatus Paul's letters do not require. (Volume 2 Chapter 22, "Marcion's Evangelion")

- Mark, the earliest canonical gospel, independently converges with the Evangelion: no birth narrative, Jesus appearing as an adult, authority from nowhere within the Jewish system, an empty tomb ending with terrified silence and no physical resurrection appearance. The Gospel of Thomas converges from a third independent direction – sayings without system, salvation through recognition rather than sacrifice, no Jewish continuity apparatus. Three independent early streams of tradition arriving at the same position. (Volume 2 Chapters 20, 21)
- The unknown Father's governing logic is most directly stated in the love-your-enemies saying securely attested in Marcion's Evangelion (Luke 6:27-35): the Father makes his sun rise on the evil and the good and sends rain on the just and the unjust. The reach is unconditioned, addressed to everyone, present before any account of merit is rendered. That is grace as the prior reality, not mercy as the after-the-fact softening of judgement. (Volume 2 Chapter 22, "Marcion's Evangelion")
- The Χρηστός/Χριστός distinction – a single vowel, η versus ι – is a window onto the editorial programme rather than an encoding of the whole thesis. Chrestos means the good one. Christos means the anointed covenant fulfiller. Suetonius – the Roman biographer of the Caesars, writing in early-second-century Latin, where the Koine η/ι phonetic merger of Greek does not apply – recorded the movement in 49 CE as Chrestos. Early manuscripts preserve the η spelling. Itacism (the Koine merger) accounts for some of the η/ι scatter inside the Greek manuscript tradition; what does not fit a random-confusion account is the directional pattern of standardisation toward Christos, which fits the Catholicising programme this volume documents elsewhere. The vowel does not by itself prove the case. It indexes it. (Volume 2 Chapter 28, "Χρηστός vs Χριστός")
- Isaiah 53 describes the Creator's sacrificial mechanism at maximum intensity – the most innocent offered to complete the highest transaction. The Marcionite inversion: the Creator completed his transaction, but what he received was a seed. What seeds do when they die is not complete a transaction. It is begin a distribution. (Volume 2 Chapter 29, "Isaiah 53")

The asymmetry worth noting: the orthodox framework had custody of the manuscripts and the power to define the canon. The transaction/grace contrast survives only in the quotations of its opponents and in stone inscriptions buried in Syria. When one side has controlled the archive for two thousand years, the weight of manuscript evidence and institutional continuity is not straightforwardly neutral. This is the argument the rest of the document develops. The evidence is there. The reader decides what weight to give it.

The transaction/grace reading has the weight of structural anomaly, directional interpolation pattern, independent convergence across sources with no historical connection to each other, and the evidence of what was excluded from the canon. It does not have institutional continuity. It has analytical coherence and the archaeology of what was suppressed.

The orthodox reading has the weight of transmitted tradition, institutional continuity, and sheer manuscript volume. It is the default position and its default status is earned — it has been the working framework of the most serious theological minds for two millennia.

Before anything else — before Marcion, before interpolation theory, before any claim about specific passages — there is one foundational fact that must be established. It is not disputed. Every serious scholar of the New Testament accepts it.

Chapter 1
We Know Texts Were Changed

Before any argument about Paul. Before Marcion. Before interpolation theory applied to specific letters. There is a prior question that must be settled first – and it can be settled on entirely uncontested ground.

Did ancient scribes add material to the New Testament texts?

The answer is yes. This is not disputed by any serious scholar – conservative, liberal, orthodox, or secular. The evidence is in the manuscripts themselves, and it is clear enough that most modern Bible translations note it in their footnotes. What follows are three cases where the addition is universally or near-universally acknowledged. They matter not just as isolated facts but as a profile. They show what scribal addition looks like when we can prove it – so that the same profile can be recognised elsewhere. These three are among the most visible. They are not unique. Volume 2 documents five cases in full; what follows is the core profile sufficient for the argument that follows.

The Longer Ending of Mark (Mark 16:9-20)

Mark's gospel ends at verse 8. "They said nothing to anyone, for they were afraid." That is the original ending. The women flee the empty tomb in terror and tell no one. It is abrupt, unsatisfying, and theologically raw. It contains no resurrection appearances, no commission to the disciples, no ascension, no miraculous signs.

Every major Bible translation – including the most conservative – places a note at Mark 16:8 informing the reader that the verses which follow are not found in the oldest and most reliable manuscripts. Codex Sinaiticus and Codex Vaticanus, the two earliest near-complete Greek New Testaments (4th century), end Mark at verse 8. Eusebius and Jerome both note in the 4th century that the longer ending is absent from accurate copies. The shorter form is treated as original by virtually all textual scholars across the conservative to liberal spectrum. The longer ending is a 2nd-century addition.

The content of the addition is revealing. It introduces resurrection appearances, commissions the disciples, promises signs to believers — handling serpents, speaking in tongues, healing — and records an ascension. None of this is in the original eight verses. All of it serves a clear need: a gospel that ends with terrified women who tell no one is a poor foundation for a missionary movement claiming apostolic authority. The addition solves that problem.

This is what a scribal insertion looks like. The original text ends coherently — nothing in 16:1-8 requires 16:9-20 to complete it. The added material appears in later manuscripts only. It serves an identifiable institutional purpose. When you remove it, nothing is missing.

The Woman Caught in Adultery (John 7:53-8:11)

"Let him who is without sin among you be the first to throw a stone at her." This is one of the most beloved passages in the gospels. It is also, according to virtually all textual scholars across the entire tradition, not original to John.

It is absent from the oldest Greek manuscripts and from the earliest Latin, Syriac, Coptic, and Armenian translations. When it does appear in later manuscripts, it moves — some place it after John 7:36, some after John 21:25, some in Luke. A passage that floats around the manuscript tradition rather than sitting in one fixed location is almost certainly a later insertion looking for a home. The writing style differs from the surrounding chapters of John; the vocabulary is Synoptic rather than Johannine. The story may be old and may even be authentic to the gospel tradition, but it is not original to John.

The Heavenly Witnesses (1 John 5:7)

1 John 5:7 — the Comma Johanneum — is the most explicit Trinitarian statement in the New Testament: "For there are three that bear witness in heaven: the Father, the Word, and the Holy Spirit; and these three are one." It is absent from every Greek manuscript before the 16th century (with two exceptions that appear back-translated from Latin), absent from the Greek fathers, absent from the Latin fathers before the 4th century. It entered Latin manuscripts in Spain and North Africa during the Trinitarian controversies and migrated from there. Erasmus initially refused to include it in his Greek New Testament for lack of manuscript support. It is now omitted from every

modern critical edition. The doctrine of the Trinity does not depend on it, but the verse itself is a 4th-century insertion.

What These Cases Share

Three cases. Three different books. Additions ranging from a single inserted verse to a block of narrative. All three are now acknowledged by the overwhelming consensus of scholarship across denominations, across theological commitments, across continents.

What they share is a recognisable profile. The added material is absent from the oldest and most authoritative manuscripts and appears first in later witnesses. The surrounding text forms a complete unit without it – removing the addition leaves clarity, not a gap. The addition serves a specific and identifiable institutional need of the period in which it appears. Where writing style can be tested, it differs from the surrounding text. The insertion point is often unstable – the material moves between manuscripts rather than sitting firmly in a single location.

This profile is not invented here. It is the standard set of criteria textual scholars have used for two centuries to identify late additions across ancient texts – Homer, Plato, Josephus, Tacitus, and the New Testament alike. It produces results that transcend theological commitments. Liberal scholars and conservative scholars, using the same methods, arrive at the same conclusions about these passages.

The question that follows is not rhetorical. It is methodological. If additions occurred – and they did – then the presence of a passage in the manuscript tradition cannot by itself establish that the passage is original. Presence means transmission. It does not mean origin. A verse can be in every manuscript from the 4th century forward and still not have been in the letter Paul wrote in 53 CE.

This changes what questions are available. Not: was this passage added? That requires proof. But: can the question of whether this passage was original be settled by its presence in manuscripts alone? After Mark 16, John 7:53-8:11, and 1 John 5:7, the answer is no. The same signal profile that identified those additions – tested on uncontested ground – is the framework applied to Paul's letters in what follows.

Chapter 2
Therefore the Question Is Open

The question runs in two directions: do any Pauline passages carry the same signal profile as the proven cases, and does an earlier gospel tradition – Marcion's Evangelion – converge with reconstructed Paul from a different direction?

Those signals are not invented for this argument. They are the same criteria that identified Mark 16, John 7:53-8:11, and 1 John 5:7 as secondary – criteria conservative and liberal scholars alike accept as legitimate.

The Signals, Applied

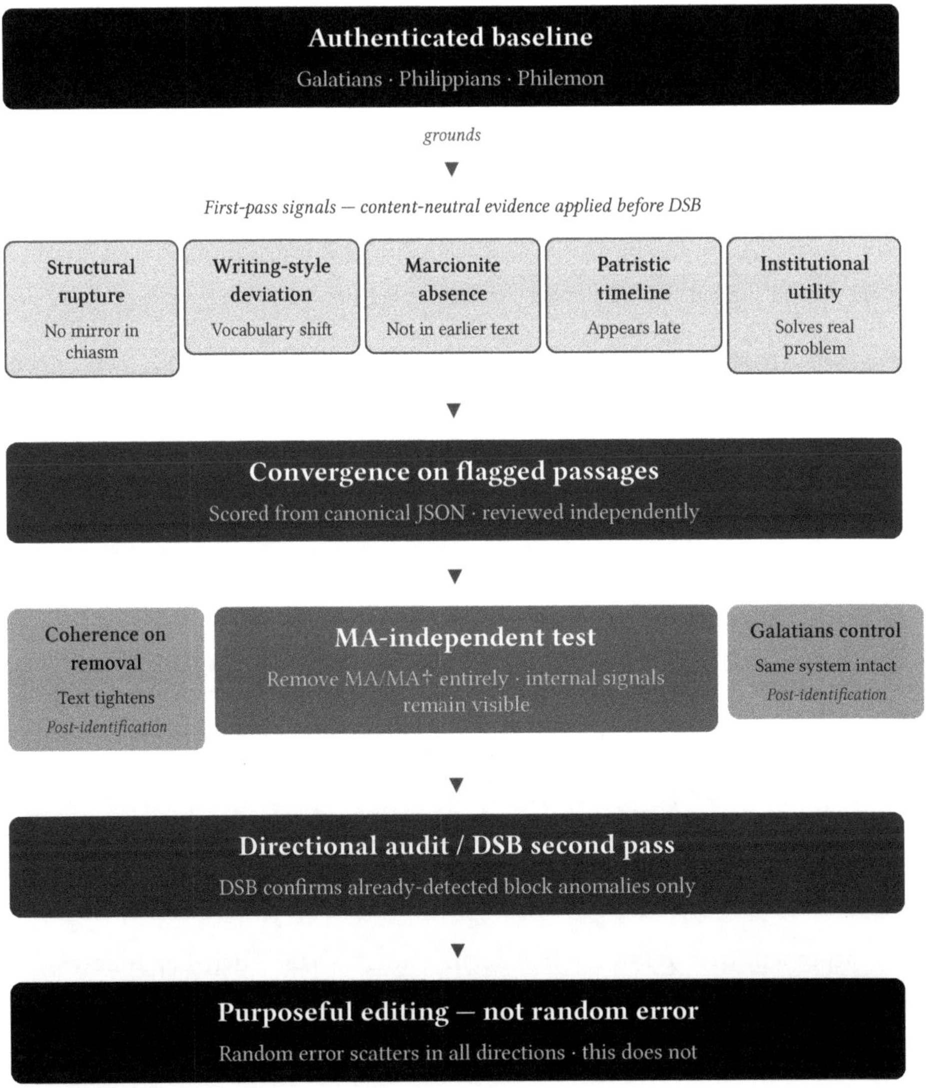

The interpolation signal system — first-pass evidence, MA-independent review, and DSB second-pass audit

From these proven cases (and the five documented in full in Volume 2), twelve signals emerge. Not all apply to every situation. Not all carry equal weight. But they form a consistent diagnostic framework — the same framework textual scholars use across all ancient literature. Applied to Paul's letters, six of the twelve are strongly operative, and two are newly identified from the proven cases that were not yet explicitly named in prior scholarship on Paul.

The six main signals are: Does the surrounding text form a complete argument without this passage? Does vocabulary or writing style shift at the passage boundary? Does the passage solve a specific institutional problem of the period when it first appears? Do writers who would have cited it if they knew it existed fail to do so? Does the passage first appear prominently at the time of the controversy it would resolve? Does it sound like a different voice rather than merely a different topic?

'Hostile witness' covers any writer who would have had reason to cite the passage if they knew of it – adversaries, allies, or neutrals, each with their own stake in the doctrine it would establish.

Two signals from the proven cases that are new to the Pauline analysis

Internal anachronism – a passage references a situation that arose after the main letter was written. 1 Thessalonians 2:14-16, which refers to "wrath that has come upon them at last" in language that echoes the destruction of Jerusalem in 70 CE, was written by Paul around 50 CE – twenty years before that event. A writer in 50 CE does not describe as complete an event that had not yet occurred. The passage shows knowledge of what happened in 70 CE. Paul did not.

Positional instability – the Romans doxology (16:25-27) – a closing formula of praise appears after chapter 14 in some manuscripts, after chapter 15 in others, and after chapter 16 in others. A passage that cannot find a stable position in the manuscript tradition is behaving exactly like John 7:53-8:11 – a passage looking for where it belongs.

The Chain of Questions

The argument that follows in this document is a chain. Each step follows from the previous one. None requires accepting the conclusion before seeing the evidence. The chain runs like this:

We know texts were changed. The signal profile tells us how to recognise when they were. So: do any passages in Paul's letters match that profile?

When the signals are applied, specific passages flag consistently – not one signal but several converging on the same text. So: what do the flagged passages have in common?

The proven cases established that ancient scribes added material – and that we can tell when they did. Now the same diagnostic framework is applied to

Paul's letters. What emerges is something that cannot be explained by random copying error.

The one-way signature

Signal Key

MA	Marcionite absence – direct or block-inherited (weight 0.75)	**MA†**	qualified Marcionite absence – indirect or contested (weight 0.65)
IA	internal anachronism / independent attestation (weight 0.9)	**SR**	structural rupture – coherence broken by passage
WS	Walker (2001) vocabulary and linguistic identification	**AC**	argument completes without passage
HS	hostile silence – fathers argue past passage without quoting	**HW**	hostile awkward defence – argument weakened by passage
TC	temporal correlation – anachronistic content	**PI**	positional instability – floating in manuscript tradition
IU	institutional utility – passage benefits later institution (weight 0.1)	**DSB**	directional signature, block-confirming – second-pass audit confirms a first-pass block anomaly (weight 0.4)

Set aside individual verses and hold onto the broader diagnostic: the suspect passages cluster toward law affirmation, covenant continuity, Roman deference, and institutional manageability. The point is not that directionality alone proves interpolation. It is that the same direction remains visible when Marcionite Absence is removed and only structural, stylistic, patristic, and argument-completion signals are left.

This matters because of what it rules out. Random scribal copying errors do not produce one-directional results. Copying mistakes scatter changes across all directions – some making the theology harder, some easier, some more institutional, some less. Over centuries of transmission, random error produces noise distributed across the possible directions of change. What this document records is not noise. It is signal: one-directional theological drift that cannot be explained by accident. There is only one model consistent with 100% directional alignment across every identified passage: purposeful editing by people with a consistent institutional agenda. The direction of the editing is the signature of who was doing the editing and why.

This is sharpened by evidence from a different direction. Bart Ehrman, working from manuscript variants with no interest in Marcion, documented the same asymmetry in The Orthodox Corruption of Scripture (1993): proto-orthodox scribes altered New Testament texts consistently toward orthodox positions – Creator-Father identity, birth-lineage embodiment, institutional hierarchy – and never the other way. Ehrman's work covers word-level scribal alterations, not large-scale insertion; but the directional signature matches. Two scholars, different methods, the same finding.

The obvious counter-argument is that this one-way signature is exactly what Marcion's own editing would produce. The answer is that the pattern is independently reproducible without Marcion: the same passages flag on structural rupture, style anomaly, argument completion, hostile silence, and temporal correlation. Tertullian never accuses Marcion of removing the pro-Hebrew material that would have been the strongest possible charge, and across all 153 assessed passages the directional pattern has no counter-example.

A direct test is available. Volume 2 gives each flagged passage two confidence scores — one including Marcionite Absence and one excluding it entirely. Stripped of Marcion, the directional pattern still holds. Marcion is not the foundation of the argument. He is one corroborating witness among several.

The directional asymmetry has a positive counterpart. When the passages identified in this document as secondary are removed, the letters that remain are not incoherent fragments — they are thematically consistent across ten different documents written to ten different audiences on ten different occasions. Romans argues grace without law in systematic form; Galatians argues it confrontationally; Philippians lives it personally; Philemon enacts it in a single relationship; 1 and 2 Corinthians, Ephesians, Colossians, and 1 Thessalonians apply or assume it in their different contexts. Without the suspect passages, the contradiction within the canonical Pauline corpus — the Paul who abolishes the law alongside the Paul who validates it; the Paul who declares there is neither slave nor free alongside the Paul who tells slaves to obey their masters — largely disappears. What is left is one argument, made ten different ways. That coherence is either a product of circular selection, or of genuine textual stratification. The methodology addresses the circularity objection in full. The coherence itself is an observable fact about the reconstructed text that the reader can verify in Companion B.

> What would count against the interpolation thesis: A citation from church fathers writing before Marcion (pre-Marcionite) — Christian writers before 144 CE, before Marcion became prominent, quoting one of the suspect passages in a non-polemical context would significantly weaken specific interpolation claims. Stylometric (quantitative writing-style analysis used to test authorship) analysis showing the suspect passages indistinguishable from authentic Paul would challenge the thesis. These remain possible discoveries that would require revision of specific claims. Demonstration that 1 Thessalonians 2:14-16 was written before 70 CE would eliminate the internal anachronism signal for that passage. Evidence that the Romans doxology (16:25-27) was stable in a single position before the 3rd century would eliminate the positional instability signal for that passage.

The manuscript problem

Every manuscript we have contains the Jewish material. There is no physical manuscript of a pre-interpolated Paul. This is a genuine objection. The honest answer: for over a thousand years the only people copying Paul's letters were the institution with an interest in the longer version. Absence of pre-interpolation manuscripts is consistent with suppression – but consistent with suppression is not the same as proof. Normal historical loss could account for the same absence. The manuscript question is real. It is not the argument.

The argument rests on the positive signal profile, not on manuscript absence. Think of it as diagnosing a patient: one symptom could mean many things; five symptoms from five independent specialists pointing at the same diagnosis makes coincidence very hard to sustain. The signals were developed independently by scholars who did not share the same agenda. When they converge on the same passage, the cumulative case stands on what is present, not what is missing.

> A legitimate challenge: the tests all require a baseline – a version of 'authentic Paul' to compare against. If the baseline is chosen by excluding suspect passages, the analysis risks circularity. The baseline here is Galatians, Philippians, and Philemon, selected on three independent grounds that do not depend on the transaction/grace reading: early and consistent patristic attestation before any anti-Marcionite consolidation; zero instances of the vocabulary patterns concentrated in contested sections; and uncontested scholarly consensus on authenticity. The Romans ring composition is identifiable from compositional analysis alone – the disrupted symmetry falls out of the structure, not the theology. The framework is tested against these independent signals. It does not generate them.

The Canon Itself Rests on the Same Structure

The circularity objection – that this document identifies authentic Paul as the Paul who sounds Marcionite and then flags non-Marcionite passages as interpolations – is a genuine methodological concern and this document has acknowledged it. But the objection applies with equal force to the evidence base against which this methodology is being measured. The New Testament canon, the manuscript tradition that preserved it, and the patristic consensus that defined its boundaries all rest on the same circular structure the critique identifies here.

The canon was assembled by communities that already held specific theological commitments – that Jesus was the fulfilment of Hebrew prophecy, that the God of Israel and the Father of Jesus were the same, that apostolic authority ran through Jerusalem and Rome. The criteria for canonicity were explicitly theological: apostolic authorship, orthodox doctrinal content, and catholic use by communities already committed to the emerging orthodox framework. Texts that confirmed those prior commitments were preserved. Texts that challenged them were destroyed or suppressed. The Marcionite texts, the Gospel of Thomas, the Gospel of Peter – inclusion or exclusion was determined by theological coherence with a framework that preceded the selection process.

> The editorial programme ran in both directions simultaneously. Within surviving texts, passages were added – the verse-level interpolations this series documents across the Pauline corpus. Across the collection of documents, entire texts were suppressed or destroyed: Marcion's Antitheses (the most thoroughly lost of his works, because a document that simply places texts side by side and says 'look' has no counter-move available except destruction); the Gospel of Thomas (buried in sand around 390 CE, not recovered until 1945); the Didache (excluded from the canon despite predating most canonical texts); and 1 Enoch (quoted as authoritative prophecy in Jude 1:14 – 'Enoch, the seventh from Adam, prophesied...' – and then removed from the canon the very text that cites it). The same institutional logic governs both operations: what was added and what was preserved were what the institution needed; what was suppressed and what was removed were what it did not. The additions to Paul's letters and the exclusions from the canon are the same editorial hand working in two directions at once.

This is not a reason to dismiss the manuscript tradition. It is a reason to recognise that no methodology working on Christian origins operates from a neutral baseline. The orthodox canon was assembled by communities with theological commitments; Bart Ehrman's The Orthodox Corruption of Scripture documents that scribes altered manuscripts to bring them into closer alignment with those commitments. The transaction/grace contrast operates from a different interpretive baseline and arrives at different conclusions about the same evidence. The choice between baselines is a methodological decision that has to be argued for; neither is inherent in the manuscripts themselves.

A residual that the methodology cannot eliminate: the corpus available for analysis is the one orthodox transmission preserved, including the baseline letters. This cannot be argued away. It can only be named, bounded, and offset by the convergence of multiple independent lines of evidence. The argument is not that the residual is absent. It is that the convergence is strong enough that the residual does not realistically explain it.

One principle scopes all of the methodological objections at once. Before a single Catholicising addition is established, the default is the manuscript-faithful one: the transmitted text is presumed original, and any interpolation claim carries an exceptional burden. After even one addition is established, the default changes. The cabinet has not been broken into; the cabinet has been shown to contain forgeries – and now every other document sharing the same forensic profile carries a question it did not carry before. Not a verdict; a question. The owner is asked to justify, not simply assert. This is not special pleading. It is exactly how scholarship treats Deutero-Isaiah, Homeric interpolations, the Testimonium Flavianum, and the longer ending of Mark. No one demands independent proof from scratch of every Homeric interpolation once the first is established. The methodology is asking that the same standard be applied to Paul that is applied everywhere else. The claim is very hard to contest because it asserts no conspiracy, no blanket rejection, no foregone conclusion — only methodological consistency.

The converging signals land most dramatically on one letter: Romans. And Romans contains a structural anomaly so specific it can be mapped architecturally.

The structural evidence — Romans as a test case

Romans exhibits what appears to be a ring composition structure — an ancient literary device where sections mirror each other concentrically toward a central point. Ancient texts were not always perfectly symmetrical and the ring composition model is one scholarly interpretation among several. What the model does is provide an independent structural framework against which anomalies can be measured — and where structural anomaly, writing-style deviation (stylometric deviation), and patristic citation patterns converge on the same passages, the cumulative case becomes more substantial than any single signal alone.

Think of it like a mirror placed at the centre of a sentence. The sentence reads the same from both ends toward the middle. In a text-length chiasm, section A at the start mirrors section A' at the end; section B mirrors B'; and so on inward until the central section — the one with no mirror — is the point the whole structure is built around. Hebrew and Hellenistic authors used this device extensively. The Psalms use it. Homer uses it. Paul uses it in several letters. When a text is organised this way, a section that disrupts the symmetry — that has no corresponding mirror, or whose mirror is disproportionately long — is structurally anomalous in a way that is visible before any theological argument is made about it.

Before the map: one mirror pair in plain English. The opening of Romans (chapters 1–4) and the closing of Romans (chapters 15–16) are mirror images. Both discuss Paul's mission to the Gentiles. Both describe the gospel reaching the ends of the earth. The beginning sets up what the end fulfils. That is what a chiasm does. Now notice what the mirror structure is arranged — the point at the centre of the letter, the thing everything else is pointing toward: chapter 8. No condemnation. Spirit adoption. Nothing separating us from the love of God. Then look at what sits immediately on either side of that centre: chapters 7 and 9–11 — the passages this document identifies as the most likely insertions. If the structure is a mirror and the centre is chapter 8, chapters 7 and 9–11 do not belong in the design. They interrupt it.

The ring structure of Romans

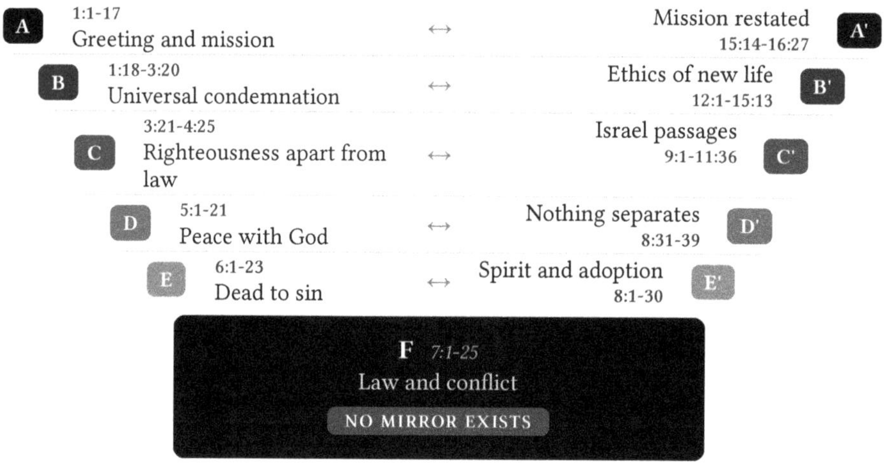

F (7:1-25) — Law and conflict

This is the point where the argument requires the most careful thought. The absence of a mirror for Romans 7 is not by itself proof of interpolation. Authors break their own structures. Chiasms are rarely perfect across long compositions. But the signal does not rest on chiastic disruption alone: Romans 7 also flags on writing-style deviation, on the abrupt shift to a positive view of the law, on the cleanness of the 6:23 → 8:1 seam when the chapter is removed, and on Marcionite Absence. The chiastic anomaly is one signal among several that converge on the same passage.

X (8:1-17) — THE CENTRE — No condemnation, Spirit adoption, Father's love

> The structural centre of Romans — the point toward which the architecture appears to converge — is Romans 8:1-17. No condemnation. Spirit adoption. Nothing separating from the Father's love. This reading of the ring structure is one scholarly model; others exist. What it provides is a framework for identifying where structural disruptions occur.

The Coherence Test — What Removal Produces

The interpolation methodology generates a prediction that can be tested independently of the theory that generated it. If the suspect passages are authentic Paul — if Romans 7, Romans 9–11, and Romans 13:1–7 were always part of the letter — then removing them should produce incoherent text. Arguments should be interrupted mid-thought. Transitions should break. The letter should read like a document with pages torn out.

This is not what the reconstructed Apostolikon (Marcion's ten-letter collection of Paul's letters) produces. The reconstruction presented in Companion B (The Apostolikon) was assembled by lifting the suspect passages out and replacing them with markers. No bridging text was written. No transitions were composed. No editorial work was done to make the remaining text flow. The joins were left wherever they fell. The result was then read from start to finish to assess whether it cohered.

It coheres. More than that: in several places it coheres more tightly without the suspect passages than it does with them. Romans 6 ends at 6:23 — "the wages of sin is death, but the free gift of God is eternal life in Christ Jesus our Lord" — and Romans 8 opens at 8:1 — "there is therefore now no condemnation for those who are in Christ Jesus." The connection is immediate and logical. Romans 6 established that the believer is dead to sin and alive to God. Romans 8 states the consequence: no condemnation. The "therefore" at 8:1 is earned by the argument of chapter 6. Romans 7 — the law-and-conflict chapter between them — interrupts this connection. With it removed, "therefore" lands where Paul intended it to land.

The same test applied to Galatians produces the same result. Galatians requires almost no reconstruction. It is the control case — the letter scholars are most confident is uninterpolated, the letter with no section flagged for removal in the reconstruction. Galatians reads as a single sustained argument from first verse to last: Paul's independent authority, the confrontation at Antioch, the grace-not-law argument, the practical ethics of the Spirit. No joins. No interruptions. The theological system that emerges from Galatians and the theological system that emerges from reconstructed Romans are identical. This is the independent convergence argument. Two letters, one producing the system intact and the other producing it only after reconstruction, arriving at the same place.

The coherence test matters because it was not used to identify the passages in the first place. The interpolation thesis was developed through structural disruption, writing-style deviation, patristic citation timeline, theological tension, and Marcionite attestation. Argument completion without the passage tests what happens afterward. When removal produces a tighter text rather than a gapped one, that is a seventh signal confirming the thesis rather than generating it.

The clearest example is Romans 12:1. In the canonical text the "therefore" has to reach back across Romans 9–11. Without those chapters it refers directly to Romans 8:38–39, and the connection is immediate: because nothing separates you from that love, present yourselves as a living sacrifice.

The counter-argument must be stated: coherence after removal could be explained by Paul's compositional habits rather than by interpolation. Paul repeats themes. He returns to the grace argument from multiple angles. Any section removed from a densely argumentative letter might leave the surrounding material still coherent, simply because the material was redundant. This is a legitimate objection and it has partial force.

The response is specific rather than general. Romans 7 is not a thematic repetition that could be removed without disruption – it is the only section of Romans that presents a positive view of the law, directly contradicting the surrounding material. Its removal does not simply leave the argument intact; it removes the argument's most acute internal contradiction. Romans 9–11 is not background material – it is three full chapters of dense theological content whose removal leaves the letter moving from chapter 8 to chapter 12 without any content gap in the argument Paul was making. He finished the grace argument in chapter 8. He begins the ethical conclusion in chapter 12. The material between them is not required by the argument on either side of it. If it were original, its absence would be felt. It is not felt.

The same comparison can be made against the Evangelion evidence, but it should not be overstated. The series no longer reproduces a full in-house gospel reconstruction. The relevant point is narrower and stronger: the published scholarly reconstructions of BeDuhn and Roth show a Luke-family gospel, known through hostile witnesses, whose most secure differences from canonical Luke cluster around Hebrew-continuity apparatus – birth narrative, genealogy, prophetic preparation, and post-resurrection scripture-fulfilment material. That pattern converges with the Pauline reconstruction without requiring the reader to accept every verse-level inference.

The coherence of the reconstruction is evidence. It is not proof. Coherence is compatible with the alternative explanation – that Paul happened to write a coherent letter even including the passages under suspicion, and that the passages removed happened to be dispensable rather than intrusive. The document does not claim more than the evidence supports. What it claims is this: the predicted outcome of the interpolation thesis – that removal of the suspect passages would leave a more coherent, not less coherent, text – was confirmed when the reconstruction was assembled and read. That confirmation is a seventh signal, independent of the five used to identify the passages. Seven independent signals pointing in the same direction constitute a cumulative case that is harder to explain away than any single signal alone.

A Concrete Example: Romans 6 → 8 Without Chapter 7

The most accessible way to see the coherence claim is to read the seam itself.

Romans 6 ends: "For the wages of sin is death, but the free gift of God is eternal life in Christ Jesus our Lord." (Rom 6:23)

Romans 8 begins: "There is therefore now no condemnation for those who are in Christ Jesus." (Rom 8:1)

Read those two sentences in immediate succession. The argument moves directly from death-and-gift to no-condemnation. The transition is theological and complete: the wages of sin are death, but the gift is eternal life — therefore no condemnation now.

Now insert Romans 7 between them. Read 6:23, then chapter 7 in full ("the law is spiritual, but I am of the flesh, sold under sin... O wretched man that I am!"), then 8:1. Notice what happens. The introspective Jewish-law lament is a 25-verse interruption between two sentences that already complete each other. The "therefore" of 8:1 no longer has anything immediately preceding it to be the consequence of.

This is what the coherence test looks like in operation. It is not proof on its own. It is one observation of the kind the volume runs systematically across the Pauline corpus.

What Would Disprove This

The argument made here is testable. Each of the following findings would defeat it, and the methodology is structured so that each can be checked independently.

1. **A pre-Marcionite citation.** If a Christian writer before 144 CE quotes one of the suspected interpolated passages — Romans 7, Romans 9–11, Romans 13:1–7, 1 Corinthians 14:34–35, 2 Corinthians 6:14–7:1, 1 Thessalonians 2:14–16 — then the passage existed in Paul's letters before Marcion could have removed it. The interpolation thesis for that passage fails. (Polycarp's c. 130 CE citation of Philippians is exactly the kind of evidence that would defeat a case for interpolating Philippians. No equivalent evidence exists for the suspect passages.)
2. **A directional counter-example.** If a single flagged passage moves Paul away from law-affirmation, covenant continuity, or institutional hierar-

chy — toward radical grace — the directional-asymmetry argument breaks. Every flagged passage must, on the thesis, point the same way. A genuine counter-example would show that the pattern is not pattern but coincidence.

3. **Coherence collapse on removal.** If removing the suspect passages produces incoherence — broken sentences, abandoned arguments, theology that does not fit Galatians and Philippians — then the suspect passages are doing essential work and the case for their interpolation fails. The reconstructed Apostolikon (Companion B) and the verse-by-verse adjudication record (Companion A) are presented precisely so this test can be run by any reader.
4. **An equally strong directional pattern in Galatians or Philippians.** If Galatians or Philippians — the control letters — show the same accumulated drift toward law-positive material, the comparison that anchors the analysis dissolves. The control-versus-treated distinction has to hold for the methodology to be valid.

These conditions are not rhetorical. They are the points at which the argument can be tested and broken. Volume 2 examines each one across 153 assessed passages.

Marcion's Evangelion — A Second Witness Converging

The Pauline letters are not the only source. Marcion also carried a gospel — reconstructed by scholars from hostile witnesses rather than preserved in manuscript form — whose secure profile converges with reconstructed Paul in ways that could not have been engineered by this series. The forensic Pauline detail lives in Volume 2; what follows here is the second half of the brief form's case, the gospel tradition that runs in parallel.

What BeDuhn's reconstruction reveals

Jason BeDuhn's reconstruction of Marcion's Evangelion in The First New Testament (2013) works by reversing Tertullian's *Adversus Marcionem* Book 4, which quotes Marcion's gospel extensively in order to refute it. By taking those quotations seriously as primary evidence rather than as exhibits in a prosecution, a text becomes visible.

What becomes visible is striking. Marcion's gospel begins with Jesus appearing in Capernaum in the fifteenth year of Tiberius — no birth narrative, no genealogy, no Bethlehem, no parents, no childhood. Jesus arrives as a fully formed adult from nowhere in particular, immediately teaching with authority, immediately driving out unclean spirits, immediately healing. This is not Luke with material removed. This is a gospel that never had that material. The opening is structurally identical to Mark's opening. The adult arrival without prior history. The immediate authority. The immediate action.

The opening — Jesus simply appears

The Evangelion opened approximately at what canonical Luke calls 4:31 — Jesus coming down to Capernaum, a city of Galilee. Tertullian attacks this opening in AM 4.7, which confirms it. No prior narrative. No Nazareth. No genealogy. No baptism scene establishing Jesus's relationship to John the Baptist and thereby to the Hebrew prophetic tradition. Jesus descends — κατῆλθεν — into Capernaum.

The word κατῆλθεν is worth attention. He came down. Not simply came or arrived. Came down. From where is not specified — which is precisely the Marcionite point. Jesus came down from the unknown Father's realm into the Creator's domain. The descent is not from Galilee to Capernaum geographically. It is the same descent the kenosis (Greek for "emptying" — the descent described in Philippians 2:6–11) hymn describes — from the form of God into the flesh of the Creator's world.

The fifteenth year of Tiberius is the single concrete historical marker. It grounds the Evangelion in specific time without grounding it in Jewish covenant history. Tiberius is not David. The fifteenth year is not a fulfillment of prophetic timetable. It is simply when it happened — the unknown Father's revealer entering the Creator's world at a specific moment in Roman imperial time, not at the culmination of Hebrew prophetic expectation.

The authority — ἐξουσία from nowhere

Luke 4:32 — and they were astonished at his teaching for his word was with authority — ἦν ὁ λόγος αὐτοῦ ἐν ἐξουσίᾳ. This is attested in Marcion's gospel. The ἐξουσία — authority, power, the right to act — is the defining characteristic of Marcion's Jesus from the first moment of his appearance.

The contrast the text draws is with the scribes. The scribes derived their authority from the tradition — from the chain of interpretation going back to Moses, from their credentials within the Creator's religious system. Jesus's authority came from nowhere within that system. It was simply present. Not derived. Not credentialed. Not authorised by any prior framework.

This is the unknown Father's operation in miniature. The unknown Father has no prior claim within the Creator's system. He arrives without credentials within that system's framework. His authority is his own nature — not delegated, not derived, not recognisable by the Creator's system as legitimate. And yet unmistakably present.

The unclean spirit — Creator's world recognising the threat

Luke 4:33-37 — the man with an unclean spirit in the synagogue. This is attested in Marcion's gospel. The unclean spirit cries: let us alone — τί ἡμῖν καὶ σοί — what is there between us and you? I know who you are — the holy one of God.

The Creator's world knows who Jesus is before any human being does. The unclean spirit — an element of the Creator's own domain — recognises the unknown Father's revealer immediately and is terrified. The humans are astonished. The Creator's spirit-world is afraid.

This reversal is theologically precise in the transaction/grace reading. The Creator's cosmic forces recognise what the Creator's human institutions cannot — that something has entered their domain that does not belong to it. The synagogue congregation is astonished by the authority. The unclean spirit is afraid of the authority. Two different levels of recognition at the first appearance.

The exorcism that follows is significant. Jesus commands — ἐπετίμησεν — be silent and come out. The unclean spirit obeys. Not because Jesus is operating within the Creator's exorcism system. Because what came from outside the Creator's domain has authority over what is inside it. The unknown Father's presence is operating within the Creator's domain from the first encounter.

Luke 10:21-22 — the hidden Father revealed

This passage is among the most theologically significant in Marcion's Evangelion and is attested clearly through Tertullian. In the Evangelion version: Ἐν αὐτῇ τῇ ὥρᾳ ἠγαλλιάσατο τῷ πνεύματι ὁ Ἰησοῦς — in that same hour Jesus rejoiced in the Spirit — and said: I acknowledge you Father Lord of heaven and earth that you have hidden these things from the wise and intelligent and revealed them to babes. Yes Father because it seemed good in your sight.

Then immediately: All things have been handed over to me by my Father – and no one knows who the Son is except the Father – and who the Father is except the Son and anyone to whom the Son wishes to reveal him.

This is the most Johannine saying in the synoptic tradition – the exclusive mutual knowledge of Father and Son, the revelation of the Father through the Son as the only access point. And it is attested in Marcion's Evangelion.

The theological structure is precisely Marcionite. The Father has hidden – ἀπέκρυψας – these things from the wise and intelligent. The unknown Father is hidden from those operating within the Creator's wisdom framework. He is revealed – ἀπεκάλυψας – to babes. Not to the credentialed, the institutionally recognised, the theologically trained. To the simple. To those who are not operating within the Creator's wisdom system.

No one knows who the Father is except the Son and anyone to whom the Son wishes to reveal him. The Father is not accessible through natural theology – through the Creator's creation witnessing to its maker. The Father is not accessible through Hebrew scripture – through the Creator's covenant tradition pointing toward its God. The Father is accessible only through the Son's deliberate act of revelation – ἀποκαλύψαι – unveiling. This is the foundational Marcionite claim expressed in Jesus's own words as attested in his own gospel.

The Good Samaritan – grace without covenant

The parable of the Good Samaritan in Luke 10:25-37 has contested Marcionite attestation – Tertullian discusses it in AM 4.27 but the discussion is complex and scholars disagree about whether it was present in Marcion's version. If present it is one of the most significant parables for the transaction/grace contrast.

A man going down from Jerusalem is beaten, robbed, and left half dead. A priest passes. A Levite passes. A Samaritan – a member of a community the Jewish tradition considered religiously compromised – stops, binds his wounds, carries him to an inn, pays for his care.

Reach before reckoning – the governing logic of the unknown Father

Grace Jesus reveals is most directly stated in a saying-cluster securely attested in Marcion's Evangelion: love your enemies, do good to those who hate you, bless those who curse you, pray for those who mistreat you. The reasoning that follows is theological – be merciful, even as your Father is merciful — for the Father makes his sun rise on the evil and the good and sends rain on the just and the unjust (Luke 6:27-36). BeDuhn's reconstruction places this saying-cluster in the Evangelion's secure core; its Marcionite attestation is not contested between the patristic witnesses.

The image is cosmological. The Father's operating logic, on this picture, is to reach everyone without first calculating who deserves it. Sun and rain arrive addressed to evil and good alike. There is no prior account of merit, no preliminary verdict, no condition that has to be met before the reach extends. The Father is, in this saying, the one who gives before the request — the gift in advance of the asking. That is what Jesus is asking his hearers to imitate: be like that — love before you check what is owed.

This is categorically different from the mercy principle within a transactional system. The Hebrew tradition contains genuine mercy material — Hosea 11, Psalm 103, the return of the exiles — but those are relational mercies inside an ongoing covenant: God relenting from a judgement the framework would otherwise require, choosing not to act according to what the covenant technically allows. What the love-your-enemies saying teaches is not relenting at all. The Father does not soften a judgement. The Father does not relent from a verdict. The Father reaches first, before the question of merit is even raised. That is the governing logic stated as principle: reach before reckoning, gift before request, the unconditioned arrival of the Father's regard.

What the Evangelion is not

Having established what the Evangelion contains and what it means, it is important to state clearly what the transaction/grace contrast does not claim about it.

The Evangelion is not a fabrication by Marcion. The passages attested in it are genuine gospel tradition — some of them among the most secure in the entire tradition. The good Samaritan. The hidden things revealed to babes. The centurion. These are not Marcionite inventions. They are gospel tradition that Marcion preserved.

The Evangelion is not a secret document with esoteric content unavailable in the canonical tradition. Everything attested in Marcion's gospel exists in canonical Luke — often in nearly identical form. What differs is what is absent. The Evangelion is a more primitive form of the same tradition — before the birth narratives, genealogies, fulfillment formulas, and Jewish continuity apparatus were added.

The Evangelion does not prove Marcion was right about everything. BeDuhn's reconstruction is a scholarly hypothesis, not a recovered text. The

Tertullian reversal methodology produces a plausible pre-Catholic gospel tradition – it does not produce a transcript of what Jesus said. The Evangelion is evidence for the Marcionite theological framework, not proof of it.

There is one more witness – discovered in Constantinople in 1873, unnoticed for nearly a thousand years. It predates the four-gospel canon. It predates institutional Christianity. And it knows nothing of what that institution would later say was always essential.

The next chapter introduces that witness.

Chapter 3
The Didache – A Witness From Before the Synthesis

In 1873, Philotheos Bryennios, Metropolitan of Nicomedia, discovered a Greek manuscript in the Jerusalem Monastery of the Most Holy Sepulchre in Constantinople. Buried inside a larger compilation dated to 1056 CE was a short text – sixteen chapters covering ethics, baptism, the Eucharist, and church order – that had been known by name to several Church Fathers but lost for centuries. Published in 1883, its full title translates: Didachē Kyriou dia tōn dōdeka apostolōn tois ethnesin – The Teaching of the Lord to the Gentiles through the Twelve Apostles. Scholars immediately recognised it as anomalous. Most now date its final form to the late first or early second century CE, with its core material possibly earlier. It is the oldest surviving Christian document outside the New Testament. What it does not contain is the argument of this chapter.

What the Didache Does Not Say

The Didache contains no crucifixion theology. It contains no resurrection theology. It contains no atonement mechanism. There is no sacrificial death of Jesus, no blood shed for sins, no legal satisfaction of a divine requirement. The Eucharistic prayers in chapters 9 and 10 – the oldest recorded Eucharistic liturgy in existence – make no mention of the Last Supper. They do not connect the cup and bread to Jesus's body and blood. They contain no institution narrative. The Eucharist in the Didache is a meal of thanksgiving for "life and knowledge" made known through Jesus – not a ritual re-enactment of a sacrifice.

There is no Johannine Logos theology. No pre-existent Word through whom all things were made. No birth-lineage theology presenting Jesus as fulfilment of Hebrew scripture. No genealogy connecting Jesus to the Davidic line as covenant fulfilment. The document is, as scholars Niederwimmer and Attridge conclude, "not a theological work but a rule for ecclesiastical praxis" — but that very absence of theology is the data. The Didachist does not feel the need to establish theological foundations that, for Paul and for the Catholicising tradition after him, were the entire point. Clayton Jefford's assessment: "There is no mention of Jesus as the Son of God or the significance of that relationship, no understanding of the nature of Jesus as preacher, healer, miracle-worker, or savior."

What the Didache Calls Jesus — Pais

The Didache does mention Jesus. It mentions him in the Eucharistic prayers, where he appears twice in close parallel. The cup prayer: "We thank thee, our Father, for the holy vine of David thy servant, which thou madest known to us through Jesus thy Servant." The bread prayer: "We thank thee, our Father, for the life and knowledge which thou madest known to us through Jesus thy Servant." The word translated Servant is pais — παῖς in Greek. It means child, servant, or intimate attendant. It is not the word for Son of God. It is not Christos in any messianic sense. It is the same word the Septuagint uses for the Isaiah 52-53 Servant figure — the suffering pais of the Lord. The Didache calls Jesus pais of the Father consistently. Not the second person of a Trinity. Not the anointed one fulfilling Hebrew prophecy. The one through whom the Father's life and knowledge were made known.

The Eucharistic prayer continues after the bread blessing: "As this broken bread was scattered over the hills and was gathered together and became one, so let thy Church be gathered together from the ends of the earth into thy kingdom." The focus is eschatological community, not sacrificial atonement. The meal is anticipatory — pointing toward a future gathering — not commemorative, not re-enacting a death. The thanks given is for life and knowledge, not for forgiveness of sins. The soteriological framework is absent because, for this community, it had not yet been constructed.

The Two Ways and the Grace Distinction

The Didache opens with the Two Ways — the Way of Life and the Way of Death. This is recognisably Jewish ethical instruction. The closest parallels are in the Dead Sea Scrolls Community Rule, where the same Two Ways framework organises the Qumran community's foundational charter. Willy Rordorf — the Swiss patristics scholar whose critical edition is the standard reference for the Didache — noted that the first five chapters of the Didache are "essentially Jewish" in structure. The ethical teaching is love of God and neighbour, avoidance of murder, adultery, theft, magic. It is the moral law of the Creator's world – the good life within the created order, conducted well. What the Didache does not do is identify this ethical instruction with the grace of the unknown Father. The ethical sections and the liturgical sections coexist without being theologically integrated in the way Paul's letters integrate them. The Didache community was doing good and giving thanks. It had not yet experienced the Pauline rupture that makes grace something categorically different from moral conduct.

The Marcionite Significance

The Didache's significance for the transaction/grace contrast operates on two levels. The first is negative: it shows that the soteriology the Catholicising tradition would later treat as foundational Christianity – the cross as sacrifice, the Eucharist as body and blood, the death and resurrection as the mechanism of salvation – was not present in at least one early Christian community that was sufficiently organised to have a liturgical manual, a baptismal practice, and a community rule. Geza Vermes calls it "priceless evidence of an undeveloped Christology." The development Vermes identifies as undeveloped is precisely what this document calls the Catholicising synthesis.

The second level is positive: the Didache's Eucharistic theology – thanks to the Father for life and knowledge made known through Jesus the pais – is theologically closer to the transaction/grace reading than to the Pauline sacrificial theology Paul himself uses. This is an important qualification. Paul's language of sacrifice and blood is one of the more awkward elements of the transaction/grace reading, addressed in Volume 2 Chapter 29, "Isaiah 53." The Didache community was not Marcionite – it was Jewish-Christian, attached to the Davidic vine, operating with a high regard for the law. But its Eucharistic centre – the Father, the pais, the transmission of life and knowledge – mirrors what a pre-Catholicising community centred on the unknown Father's revelation might look like before the sacrificial machinery was installed.

The Didache was not added to the New Testament canon. Athanasius listed it among the Apocrypha. Eusebius – the fourth-century church historian whose Ecclesiastical History is the principal narrative source for early Christianity – noted it without canonical authority. The institutional decision that excluded it is the same institutional decision that standardised the Eucharistic theology the Didache does not contain. The document that survived outside the canon preserves a liturgical practice that predates the soteriology the canon requires. The archaeology of the canon is the archaeology of what was left out.

> A concrete marker of how unsettled the canon boundary was: Jude 1:14 quotes 1 Enoch as prophecy — 'Enoch, the seventh from Adam, prophesied, saying...' — treating a non-canonical document as authoritative scripture. Jude was retained in the canon. 1 Enoch was excluded from it. The canon contains a citation of a document the canon itself removes. The editorial boundary was applied after the retained text was written, not before. This is the removal side of the same programme documented throughout this series.

The question this evidence raises is not only theological. It is historical and political. Why would the emerging institution have reattached a movement built on non-transactional grace to the Hebrew law tradition? The answer is specific — and documented.

The next chapter makes that case.

Chapter 4 Why Rome Reattached Christianity to Judaism

The argument for this has been developed in full across the relevant chapters of Volume 2. Here it is stated as a single coherent case – the institutional strategy, its mechanisms, its political logic, and the philosophical price it paid that orthodox Christianity has never resolved.

The Problem Rome Faced

By the mid-2nd century the proto-orthodox tradition in Rome faced a specific and urgent problem. Christianity had spread throughout the empire as a movement drawing primarily Gentile converts. It had no legal standing – Rome tolerated only registered religions, and Christianity was not one. It had no philosophical pedigree. It had no antiquity.

Jewish religion – despite the catastrophe of the 70 CE destruction of Jerusalem – retained the legal status of a tolerated ancient religion. Rome respected antiquity. A religion with a long history, ancient texts, and established practice had implicit legitimacy within Roman legal culture. If Christianity could establish itself as the legitimate continuation of the Hebrew tradition – as the fulfillment of ancient Jewish prophecy – it inherited Judaism's legal antiquity. It became not a new and suspicious movement but the completion of the oldest monotheistic tradition in the Roman world.

This was the political prize. The theological price was the identification of the unknown Father with the Hebrew God. The Roman institution chose institutional survival. That choice is the origin of the theological problem that has never been resolved.

The Five Mechanisms of Reattachment

The reattachment of Christianity to Judaism had already begun before any institutional mechanism was deployed. The insistence of the Jewish apostles that Jesus was the fulfillment of Hebrew prophecy, James's pressure at Antioch, the circumcision party's demand that Gentile converts enter the covenant – these were the first form of the problem, operating from within Judaism itself, a generation before Irenaeus wrote a word. What the second century added was institutional consolidation of what Jerusalem had already established theologically. Five mechanisms accomplished that consolidation simultaneously, each reinforcing the others.

The four-gospel canon established Jesus as the fulfillment of Hebrew prophecy through Matthew's saturation of fulfillment formulas, Luke's genealogy connecting Jesus to Adam and Abraham, John's identification of Jesus as the creative Logos of Genesis 1, and even Mark's citation of Isaiah in its opening verse. Each gospel contributed a different strand of Hebrew continuity. Together they surrounded the Jesus tradition with the Hebrew prophetic framework from every direction.

Acts created the fiction of apostolic continuity – Paul's gospel authorised by Jerusalem, Peter and Paul teaching the same thing, the Gentile mission growing organically from Jewish roots, the Spirit of Pentecost fulfilling Joel's prophecy. Acts is the narrative expression of the institutional strategy – a story of continuity where the authentic letters reveal rupture.

The interpolated Pauline letters embedded Hebrew continuity in Paul himself. Romans 9-11 establishing Jewish covenantal continuity. Romans 13:1-7 making Paul safe for empire. The Holy Spirit title replacing Paul's grace vocabulary with the Creator's holiness category. Paul – the apostle whose authentic letters most radically sever Christianity from the Hebrew covenant framework – was made to endorse that framework through systematic editorial addition.

The Muratorian Canon established the boundaries of acceptable scripture in direct response to Marcion's single-gospel, ten-letter canon which had no Hebrew continuity apparatus. The canonical response to Marcion was the institutional expression of the reattachment strategy – a formally defined set of documents that together made the Hebrew-continuity argument irresistible.

The genealogies are the most explicit reattachment mechanism. A genealogy is a document of belonging – placing a person within a lineage, a covenant tradition, a historical chain of inheritance. Matthew's genealogy from Abraham. Luke's from Adam. Both establish Jesus as the heir of the Creator's covenant history. Marcion's Evangelion has no genealogy in this reconstruction because the unknown Father's revealer belongs to no lineage within the Creator's world.

> Every one of the five mechanisms was directly provoked by Marcion. The four-gospel canon countered his single gospel. Acts countered his Paul-only apostolicism. The Pauline interpolations countered his letter collection. The Muratorian Canon established explicit boundaries. The genealogies embedded Jesus in the Jewish lineage he lacked in the earlier tradition. This does not require a conspiracy in the sense of coordinated secret planning. It requires institutional communities with shared theological commitments responding independently to the same threat – which is what communities do. Ehrman's documentation of scribal changes makes the same point: the scribes were not conspiring. They were copying faithfully according to their theological understanding. The systematic directional pattern is the result of shared commitments operating over time, not of any single moment of planned coordination. Institutional momentum, not conspiracy, is the right frame – and institutional momentum is actually harder to argue against because it does not require any individual to have acted in bad faith.

The Philosophical Price

The reattachment solved the legal and political problem at a philosophical cost that orthodox Christianity has never fully resolved. If the Father of Jesus is the Hebrew God then the Father who makes his sun rise on the evil and the good is the same God who ordered the destruction of the Canaanites. The Father who reaches before any account of merit is rendered is the same God who drowned Egypt. The non-transactional grace is the governing logic of the same God who threatens punishment across generations.

The orthodox tradition has spent two thousand years attempting to resolve this tension – through developmental theology, through genre distinctions, through the distinction between wrath and mercy within a single being, through the New Testament fulfilling and correcting the Old. None of these resolutions is philosophically satisfying because the problem they are trying to solve is real. Transactional logic and grace – the Creator's justice and the unknown Father's grace – are not different moods of the same being. They are categorically incompatible.

The reattachment strategy created the problem it was solving for. Rome needed Christianity to be ancient. The price of antiquity was the identification with a God whose nature is incompatible with what Jesus revealed. Every theological crisis in Christian history involving the relationship between the Hebrew scriptures and the gospel – theodicy, divine violence, the problem of evil, the tension between law and grace – is the consequence of the reattachment strategy paying its price across centuries.

Marcion's Position in Political Terms

Marcion was not making a purely theological argument. He was making a political argument with theological consequences. His position: Christianity has no need to claim the Hebrew God's antiquity because Christianity is not the continuation of the Hebrew tradition. It is the arrival of something categorically new. The unknown Father was hidden before Jesus. He has no prior history within the Creator's world. There is no antiquity to inherit.

This position sacrificed the legal protection of inherited antiquity. A Christianity with no connection to the Hebrew tradition — no prophetic pedigree, no ancient texts, no covenant lineage — was a new and legally vulnerable movement with no institutional shelter. Marcion accepted that vulnerability. Rome did not. The reattachment strategy is the choice institutional survival requires when the theological cost is not visible until later.

By the time the cost became visible — when the full incompatibility of the transactional logic and grace could not be ignored — the institutional apparatus was already built. The four gospels were canonical. The interpolated Paul was the only Paul available. Acts was the founding narrative. The creeds were established. The Muratorian Canon was the boundary. Marcion was heresy. The alternatives were suppressed.

> The reattachment strategy succeeded institutionally and failed theologically. It produced the largest religious institution in human history. It also produced the most persistently unresolved theological tension in that institution's history. The tension is not a failure of resolution. It is the cost of the choice made in Rome in the 2nd century being paid in every subsequent generation.

Chapter 5
By What Authority

The textual argument has a downstream consequence the opening sketched and this chapter now traces explicitly, link by link. If the reconstructed Pauline letters have been edited, and if the editing moves consistently in the direction of building an institutional and political architecture the original text did not authorise, then the institution that emerged from those edits sits on a foundation it cannot defend in its own terms. The same question has to be asked of every chain of authority that runs through it — including modern ones. Volume 3 makes the full case; what follows is its compressed shape.

The Same Hand, The Larger Frame

The pattern that produced the institutional Pauline corpus did not stop at the canon. The institution the edited letters underwrote went on to issue the foundational legal instruments of European colonisation — the same law-and-covenant architecture, on a different scale, across a different medium. Volume 3 traces the chain from the editorial programme described in Chapter 1 of this short form to the title deeds of settler-colonial states across the English-speaking world. The next subsection traces it explicitly.

The chain V3 traces

1 **Territorial sovereignty**
Nation-states · Crown title · treaty frameworks · European acquisition 1452–1945
documented — legal and historical record

▼

2

Doctrine of Discovery
Dum Diversas (1452) · Romanus Pontifex (1455) · Inter Caetera (1493) · Johnson v. M'Intosh (1823) · common-law adoption
documented — legal and historical record

▼

3
DISPUTED

Petrine commission
Matt 16:18–19 · absent from Mark and Luke · second-century church-organisational vocabulary
argued — textual analysis

▼

4
DISPUTED

Political Pauline texts
Rom 13:1–7 · 1 Cor 14:34–35 · household codes · Pastoral Epistles · 1 Thess 2:14–16 · flagged confirmed or probable interpolations
argued — textual analysis

▼

5

Institutional deployment
Divine right of kings · colonial authority · women's exclusion · slave-holder theology · theological antisemitism
documented — institutional use

▼

6

Suppressed counter-architecture
Gal 3:28 · Antioch confrontation · Hidden Father · custodial and relational access without institutional mediation
collateral record — what the chain suppressed

▼

7

Continuous Indigenous legal traditions
Aboriginal Lore (65,000 yr) · Great Law of Peace (12th C) · Brehon law · Kurukan Fuga (1235) · Māori tikanga · destroyed by the authority the disputed texts legitimised
collateral record — what the chain overrode

▼

8 **System's own admission**
Mabo v Queensland No 2 (1992): to examine the foundational question "would fracture the skeleton of principle which gives the body of our law its shape and consistency"
documented — legal record

▼

9 **Architecture of oaths**
Coronation · parliamentary · judicial · police · military · citizenship · bar admission · each layer held by sworn personal subjection to the claim at links 1–4
documented — structural analysis

■ Documented — legal or historical record	D Argued — textual analysis (Vols 1–2)	Collateral record — what the chain displaced

Volume 3 lays out the chain explicitly. Each link rests on the link above it, and the chain begins with material this short form has documented. Modern national sovereignty in the common-law jurisdictions rests on the constitutional settlement that created the polity; that settlement rests on the Crown's acquisition of territory; the Crown's acquisition rests on the Doctrine of Discovery; the Doctrine of Discovery is articulated in three papal bulls of the 15th century — Dum Diversas (1452), Romanus Pontifex (1455), and Inter Caetera (1493) — which authorised Christian monarchs to seize the lands of non-Christian peoples; those bulls rest on the papal authority claimed under the Petrine commission of Matthew 16:18–19 and on the Pauline material that authorises submission to governing powers in Romans 13:1–7. The Petrine commission is patristically late on the textual evidence Volume 2 develops; Romans 13:1–7 is one of the strongest interpolation cases in the entire Pauline corpus. The chain is documentable end-to-end. The textual layer this short form summarises is the foundation that everything above it rests on.

Eddie Mabo spent a decade arguing in Australian courts that his family's land on Murray Island had never been ceded. He was a gardener at James Cook University when he first raised the question with a colleague. He died of cancer in January 1992, five months before the High Court handed down the judgment that bore his name. The court found his title was real. It also found, in the majority opinion, that the Crown's original acquisition of sovereignty over the continent was 'not justiciable before the courts.' The claim had been won. The foundation it rested on could not be examined.

The chain is enforced in actual case law. Mabo v Queensland (No 2) (Australia, 1992) names the principle directly: the Crown's acquisition of sovereignty over a territory is "not justiciable before the municipal courts." Cherokee Nation v Georgia (United States, 1831), Coe v Commonwealth (Australia, 1979), Manuel v Attorney-General (United Kingdom, 1983), and Madzimbamuto v Lardner-Burke (Privy Council, 1969) reach the same result on different facts in different jurisdictions across four centuries. The cases enforce the architecture; they do not examine its foundation. They cannot. The court's authority to sit depends on the foundation being treated as settled.

The Question the System Cannot Answer

Each link in the chain rests on the link above it. National sovereignty rests on the colonial grant that established the polity. The colonial grant rests on the papal bulls. The bulls rest on the institutional church's claim to universal jurisdiction. That claim rests on the canon and the patristic settlement — the very texts the reconstruction shows were edited. By what authority runs all the way to the foundation, and the foundation is the disputed thing. Asked the question directly, the modern system declares it non-justiciable: a court cannot examine the legitimacy of the sovereignty from which its own authority derives. That is a conclusion about power, not about law.

The hostile-witness layer

> The names and cases in this section are not required knowledge. They are the legal tradition's own canonical textbooks and judgments, cited at their word. The point is that the system's own authorities describe a foundational limit they cannot examine within the system — in plain terms, in the standard texts. No legal background is needed to follow the argument.

The standard texts of constitutional and administrative law describe the architecture openly, in their own canonical doctrinal voices. Wade and Forsyth, Administrative Law — the standard English textbook for half a century — calls parliamentary sovereignty "the ultimate political fact upon which the whole system of legislation hangs" and notes that the doctrine "is a principle of the common law and is in that sense beyond legal control." Dicey, the canonical 19th-century articulation, treats parliamentary sovereignty as the constitution's foundational rule. H. L. A. Hart's The Concept of Law grounds the entire system in a "rule of recognition" which is itself, by Hart's own account, neither valid nor invalid — it simply exists as social fact. Hans Kelsen calls this the *Grundnorm.* None of these writers is being cited against their own conclusions. They are describing the architecture in the discipline's standard vocabulary. What they describe — a foundational rule that cannot be examined within the system whose foundation it is — is exactly the architecture Volume 3 names. The cases enforce it; the doctrine prescribes it; the textbooks describe it. What none of them does, anywhere, is examine the foundation the architecture rests on.

Two Maxims the System Has Not Applied to Itself

Two common-law-logics are useful analogies here, and the system applies both rigorously to private parties.

The first is *nemo judex in causa sua* — no one should be a judge in their own cause. When a court declines to examine the foundation of its own jurisdiction on the ground that the examination would undermine that jurisdiction, that is a court judging in its own cause. The interest is existential. A judge with that level of interest in any other question would be required to recuse. The doctrinal answer — that *nemo judex* applies to particular judges in particular cases, not to the judiciary's relationship to its constitutional foundations — is true as a matter of how the doctrine is currently scoped. But the principle underneath it does not stop applying just because the interest is shared by every judge in the country rather than by one.

The second is *fraus omnia corrumpit* — fraud vitiates everything. If foundational instruments are alleged to have been obtained by fraud, the principle asks whether passage of time or accumulated practice can cure the defect. The system applies this kind of reasoning routinely to contracts, titles, and conveyances. The point here is not to state a legal result, but to observe that the constitutional foundation is not usually examined through the same lens.

The Architecture of Oaths

The reconstructed Paul does not authorise oath-architecture of any kind. Matthew 5:33-37 — the saying that condemns oath-taking — is preserved across the textual tradition. The institutional church inherited this material and built around it anyway: oaths of office, oaths of allegiance, oaths sworn on the canonical Bible itself. Modern judicial, military, and political oaths inherit the same architecture. They derive their binding force from a textual lineage the reconstruction shows was edited and a foundational grant the system declares non-examinable. The honest reckoning is the long-recognised right to affirm rather than swear — but the deeper reckoning is the recognition that the architecture is downstream of a structure the system cannot itself defend.

What the reconstructed Paul does to all of this

The architecture has a genealogy. Constitutional sovereignty in the Anglo-American tradition descends through the 1689 settlement, the earlier divine-right framework that the settlement secularised, and the Pauline material the divine-right framework drew on – Romans 13:1–7, 1 Peter 2:13–17, Titus 3:1. Crown sovereignty descends through the Doctrine of Discovery, the papal bulls, and the Petrine commission. Each of those Pauline and patristic anchors is identified in this short form as compositionally late or as one of the strongest interpolation cases in the corpus. What the reconstructed Paul actually says is the opposite of what the architecture took from him: 'For freedom Christ has set us free; do not submit again to a yoke of slavery' (Galatians 5:1); 'you were bought with a price; do not become slaves of human masters' (1 Corinthians 7:23); 'do not be conformed to this world' (Romans 12:2); 'there is neither Jew nor Greek, slave nor free' (Galatians 3:28). The implication is structural rather than personal. Wade, Dicey, Hart, and the judges in Mabo and the rest are inheritors, not architects. They are transmitting an architecture whose original theological warrant does not survive textual examination. The court's procedural decision not to examine the foundation does not change the textual fact that the foundation is documented and traced. The court's silence is a constitutive fact about the court, not about the foundation.

Where This Leads

This is the institutional implication of the textual argument. It is not a reform proposal. It is the observation that the editorial programme described in this short form has consequences that run through the modern legal and political world, and that the system has, by its own admitted standards, no answer to the foundational question. Volume 3 – The Chain from Scripture to Sovereignty – sets the case out in full: the colonial chain (the Doctrine of Discovery, Cook's Secret Instructions, terra nullius, Mabo, the Vatican's 2023 statement), the editorial pattern that produced the institutional substrate, the oath architecture, and the maxims the system applies to everyone except itself.

The textual work this short form summarises is therefore not outside the legal conversation. It is the route the procedural architecture has not closed. A court can decline to examine the sovereignty from which its own authority derives. It cannot prevent the underlying scriptures from being read. When the Pauline reconstruction is followed, the patristic timeline traced, and the editorial programme observed, the foundation the chain rests on is documented — and the documentation, traced to its origin, dissolves in the way this volume has set out. The system has a procedure for not answering the foundational question. It has no procedure for keeping the question from being asked.

Readers who hold or have held a sworn or affirmed office will find a specific note on this question at the end of Volume 3.

That implication closes the textual argument's outward arc. What remains is the inward one — the question of what to do with all of this once it has been seen.

Common Objections

A short, honest treatment of the questions a careful reader will have at this point. None of these objections is dismissed; each is the right question to be asking.

What about Romans 9–11? Doesn't Paul there teach Israel's continuity?

The case that Romans 9–11 is interpolated rests on three converging lines: it is the only major section of Romans that does not mirror an opposing partner in the letter's ring composition; its theology of corporate election and covenant continuity does not match the theology of the rest of the letter; and its Pauline character is independently questioned by William O. Walker Jr. and others. The full case is in Volume 2.

Marcion was clearly biased. Couldn't he have edited Paul to suit himself?

This is the right question to ask. Two responses. First, the directional-asymmetry observation does not depend on Marcion: every flagged passage moves in the same direction whether or not Marcion is consulted. Second, the methodology is now testable: each flagged passage in the full Apostolikon analysis carries two confidence scores, one with the Marcionite evidence included and one without it. The interpolation pattern survives without Marcion. He is one corroborating witness, not the foundation.

There is no manuscript of Paul without these passages. Doesn't that settle it?

The earliest substantial Pauline manuscripts date from the third and fourth centuries — long after the Catholicising tradition had taken physical custody of the text. The proven-interpolation cases of Chapter 1 (Mark 16:9–20, John 7:53–8:11, 1 John 5:7) demonstrate that absence of an "earlier" manuscript does not, by itself, decide the question of originality. The question is settled by the convergence of multiple independent signals, not by manuscript volume alone.

My tradition has held this text as scripture for two thousand years. Why should I take this seriously?

This argument is not addressed to people who have already decided. It is addressed to anyone who has felt the tension this volume opens with and been told not to ask. Tradition is real. The cost of revisiting inherited frameworks is real. This document is not asking for immediate capitulation. It is asking for honest inquiry.

Even if all of this is correct, what does it actually change?

That is the question Volume 3 takes up. The textual argument has institutional consequences, and the institutional consequences have legal and political consequences, because the chain of authority that produced the modern international order traces through the same editorial programme described here. The textual argument is the door. What follows depends on whether the door is opened.

A Final Word

Marcionism cannot be systematised without betraying itself.

This document is itself a system. Forty-nine chapters of organised argument, a classification apparatus for authentic and interpolated scripture, a defined vocabulary, a set of positions the reader is invited to consider. The Final Word says the moment you build a system you have re-entered transactional logic's logic. The document cannot escape this by acknowledging it. The tension is real and it does not dissolve.

What can be said is this: a map is not the territory. A description of grace, however systematic, is not grace itself. The document is an attempt to articulate something that exceeds articulation — knowing that the attempt is compromised by its own medium. The alternative is silence, which preserves purity at the cost of communicability. This document chose communication, accepting the compromise. A reader who finds the document's system-building incompatible with its own conclusions has identified something the document cannot resolve, only acknowledge.

The moment you build an institution, a ritual system, a hierarchy, a set of required beliefs, a mechanism of salvation — you have re-entered the Creator's transactional logic. This is why Marcionism was always philosophically unstable as an institution. Its own truth principle resists institutionalisation.

This document is therefore not a catechism. It is not a membership document. It is not the correct transaction/grace position that must be accepted to receive the unknown Father's grace.

What this document attempts is simply to document one honest path through the questions — the path that arrived at this position through sustained inquiry and genuine contest rather than through being handed a tradition to inherit.

The journey moved through the textual evidence — Romans ring composition, the suspected interpolations, the patristic timeline, the Tertullian reversal. Through the Greek text — the seed that dies to multiply, the untimely appearance on the Damascus road, the no condemnation of the structural centre, the Abba cry as the earliest recoverable Jesus tradition. Through the gospel tradition – Mark's adult-appearing urgent Jesus, Thomas's sayings without system, Marcion's Evangelion that never had the birth narratives that were later added to it. Through Job standing at the threshold. Through the seed and descent logic. Through the single vowel – η versus ι – that carries the entire argument compressed into one editorial choice.

One finding carries more weight than any other: the one-way pattern the earlier chapters established and confirmed at each stage examined. Every change moves in the same direction. Not one goes the other way. That pattern is the argument's signature.

If something in these pages resonates – it is not because this document is authoritative. It is because something already present within you recognised itself. If nothing here resonates, either the case has not been made compellingly enough on the evidence presented, or the lens this document offers is not the one through which the textual evidence is best read. Both are honest readings. The textual claims remain checkable on their own terms either way.

That recognition is the thing. Not the document.

On Whose Shoulders

This volume builds on a long tradition of careful scholarly work, none of which arrived at the synthesis presented here, all of which made it possible to make the argument at all. Several debts in particular.

Adolf von Harnack (1851–1930), whose 1921 monograph Marcion: Das Evangelium vom fremden Gott (Marcion: The Gospel of the Strange God) remains the foundational reconstruction effort and whose intellectual honesty about the cost of orthodoxy's victory has not been improved upon.

William O. Walker Jr. (b. 1932), whose Interpolations in the Pauline Letters (2001) developed the methodological framework on which the textual analysis here depends and demonstrated systematically that interpolation can be detected in Paul on textual grounds alone.

Bart D. Ehrman (b. 1955), whose The Orthodox Corruption of Scripture documents at length the practice of theologically motivated scribal alteration that grounds the conceptual possibility of the present case.

Jason BeDuhn, whose The First New Testament: Marcion's Scriptural Canon (2013) is the standard scholarly reconstruction of Marcion's Apostolikon and Evangelion, and the basis for this volume's treatment of Marcion's text.

Matthias Klinghardt, whose Das älteste Evangelium und die Entstehung der kanonischen Evangelien (2015) represents the most thorough recent argument that Marcion's Evangelion preserves the earliest gospel form.

The disagreements between these scholars are real. None of them would necessarily endorse the synthesis presented here. The synthesis is the responsibility of this volume; the scholarship that made it possible is theirs.

If You Want More

This short form covers the argument's shape. It does not cover the evidence in full. The complete case – forty-nine chapters, over 150 assessed passages, and the complete patristic timeline – is Volume 2: By What Authority – How Paul's Letters Were Edited. The institutional and political implication summarised in this short form is set out in full in Volume 3: By What Authority – The Chain from Scripture to Sovereignty.

If you found yourself pushing back – on the circularity of the method, the absence of pre-interpolation manuscripts, Romans 9–11 as structurally central, or Paul's own monotheism passages – those objections are engaged directly in Volume 2 Chapter 49, "The Strongest Objections", which works through sixteen of them in full. They are worth reading before you decide.

Companion A: By What Authority – The Verse-by-Verse Analysis presents the verse-by-verse adjudication with the manuscript-witness appendix and the methodology, Philemon-control, and editorial-unit appendices. Companion B: By What Authority – The Reconstructed Pauline Letters presents the Pauline corpus as a clean reading text with the interpolations removed.

The argument stands or falls on the evidence in Volume 2. This volume was only ever the door.

A Final Note

This argument was assembled to be examined, not accepted. If the textual case holds under your scrutiny – if the signals point where they seem to point and the questions seem worth asking – the most useful thing you can do is put it in front of someone else who will look at it carefully. A scholar, a lawyer, a journalist, a teacher, a friend who pushes back hard.

The argument does not need belief. It needs readers who will test it. The work of passing it on is yours to do or not.

Appendix: Glossary

Full definitions for each technical term used in this volume. Each term is also briefly defined in parentheses at its first use in the text. Return here for the fuller context.

Apostolikon — Marcion's ten-letter collection of Paul (Galatians, 1–2 Corinthians, Romans, 1–2 Thessalonians, Laodiceans [≈ Ephesians], Colossians, Philippians, Philemon), reconstructed primarily from Tertullian's quotations.

Catholicising — used here in its original sense ("making universal/orthodox"), to describe the second- and third-century editorial programme that brought the Pauline and gospel material into line with proto-orthodox theology. It does not refer specifically to the modern Roman Catholic Church.

Evangelion — Marcion's single gospel, related closely to canonical Luke but lacking the birth narrative, the genealogy, and the Hebrew-continuity material; reconstructed by BeDuhn (2013) and others.

Interpolation — a passage inserted into a text by a later editor and absent from the earlier form of that text. The Pauline examples in this volume (Romans 7, Romans 9–11, Romans 13:1–7, 1 Corinthians 14:34–35, 2 Corinthians 6:14–7:1, 1 Thessalonians 2:14–16) are the principal cases.

Kenosis — Greek for "emptying." The technical name for the descent described in Philippians 2:6–11: the celestial being empties himself of divine status and is encountered in the human condition.

Marcionite Absence (MA) — the condition in which a passage in the canonical Pauline letters is absent from Marcion's Apostolikon as reconstructed from the patristic record. One of the five interpolation signals used in this work.

Patristic — pertaining to the "Church Fathers," the second- to fifth-century Christian writers

	(Tertullian, Irenaeus, Origen, Epiphanius, etc.) whose works are the main external witness to the texts of the New Testament before the great fourth-century manuscripts.
Proto-orthodox	Bart Ehrman's term for the second- and third-century Christian groups whose theology eventually became the Nicene orthodoxy. Used here to distinguish the editorial actors from the later institutional church they produced.
Stylometry	quantitative analysis of writing style (sentence length, vocabulary distribution, function-word frequency, etc.) used to test whether a passage matches the surrounding author's habits or breaks from them.
Transaction-and-grace framework	the reading defended in this volume: that the New Testament material describes a categorical incompatibility between transactional logic and grace (transactional logic of law and covenant, and the non-transactional grace of the unknown Father), and that the institutional tradition has obscured the second by editing the first back into the texts that originally contrasted them.

Key Dates

A short orientation timeline. The full timeline is Volume 2 Chapter 38, "The Patristic Timeline".

c. 50–60 CE	Paul writes his authentic letters.
c. 49 CE	Suetonius records the disturbances in Rome under "Chrestus," the earliest external reference to the movement.
c. 70 CE	The Gospel of Mark is composed, the earliest of the canonical gospels.
c. 100 CE	The Didache is in circulation, with no cross soteriology and no canonical-Pauline framework.

c. 130 CE	Polycarp of Smyrna cites Philippians, before the anti-Marcionite consolidation.
c. 144 CE	Marcion is excommunicated in Rome and publishes his Apostolikon (a ten-letter collection of Paul) and Evangelion (a single gospel).
c. 180 CE	Irenaeus's Against Heresies fixes the four-gospel canon as the orthodox response.
c. 207 CE	Tertullian writes Against Marcion in five books, preserving the Marcionite text in the act of attacking it.
c. 367 CE	Athanasius's 39th Festal Letter fixes the New Testament canon in essentially its modern form.

www.ingramcontent.com/pod-product-compliance
Lightning Source LLC
La Vergne TN
LVHW051043210926
848486LV00001B/8